BOSS 351

MUSTANG

GTO

Nova

406

ELIMINATOR

Gran Sport

396 TURBO-JET

SUPER BEE

Powered by SRT

rally-sport

R/T

GTO 6.5 LITRE

389

ZL1

THE JUDGE

road runner

GSX

CAMARO

BOSS 302

CAMARO Z28

426HEMI

MUSCLE CARS

PAST PRESENT FUTURE

pil

Publications International, Ltd.

Louis Weber, CEO
Publications International, Ltd.
7373 North Cicero Avenue
Lincolnwood, Illinois 60712

Permission is never granted for commercial purposes.

ISBN-13: 978-1-4508-5396-5
ISBN-10: 1-4508-5396-X

Manufactured in China.

8 7 6 5 4 3 2 1

Library of Congress Control Number: 2012938147

Credits

Photography:

The editors would like to thank the following people and organizations for supplying the photography that made this book possible. They are listed below, along with the page number(s) of their photos.

Darrel Arment: 35, 66, 117, 121; **Ken Beebe:** 79, 80, 112, 130; **Mark Bilek:** 89; **Joe Bohovic:** 31, 36; **Chan Bush:** 29, 34, 67; **Jeff Cohn:** 99, 120, 126, 155, 156; **Mitch Frumkin:** 148; **Chuck Giametta:** 150; **Thomas Glatch:** 27, 67, 118; **David Gooley:** 17; **Sam Griffith:** 36, 73, 85, 120; **Jerry Heasley:** 70, 130, 146; **John Heilig:** 45; **Brandon Hemphill:** 117, 122, 131; **Milton Kieft:** 110; **Nick Komic:** 109, 115, 117, 120; **Dan Lyons:** 33; **Vince Manocchi:** 14, 15, 16, 24, 38, 39, 41, 45, 61, 64, 72, 73, 76, 81, 109, 112, 118, 121, 122, 125, 131, 134, 137, 141, 146; **Roger Mattingly:** 115, 116; **Doug Mitchel:** 15, 17, 18, 20, 22, 23, 26, 27, 28, 29, 30, 31, 32, 35, 37, 38, 39, 41, 42, 43, 60, 64, 65, 68, 72, 75, 76, 81, 89, 90, 97, 108, 112, 113, 114, 127, 129, 130, 135, 137, 138, 139, 140; **Mike Mueller:** 14, 19, 68, 109, 119, 133, 135, 136; **David Newhardt:** 71, 74, 79; **Robert Nicholson:** 119; **Rick Popely:** 88; **Al Rogers:** back cover, 18, 29, 45, 69, 71, 75, 91, 114, 116, 120, 122, 123, 124, 129, 141, 146; **Jeff Rose:** 23, 117; **Tom Shaw:** 23; **Robert Sorgatz:** 19; **Mike Spenner:** 110, 136; **Steve Statham:** 77; **Alex Steinberg:** 27; **Dennis Tanney:** 136; **David Temple:** 18, 19, 24, 29, 30, 32, 63, 113, 128, 133, 134; **Bob Tenney:** 15; **Phil Toy:** 18, 121; **Rob Van Schaick:** 25; **W. C. Waymack:** 35, 40, 62, 63, 111, 141; **Nicky Wright:** front cover, back cover, 25, 26, 28, 38, 65, 74, 128, 131, 136, 138

Owners:

Special thanks to the owners of the cars featured in this book for their cooperation.

Michael Allender: 65; **Fernando F. Alvare:** 136; **Bill Andrews:** 24; **David Arent:** front cover; **Trevor Badgley:** 131; **Vasco Baltovski:** 31; **Dennis Barnes:** 36; **Larry Bell:** back cover, 25, 28; **Benchmark Classics/Justin Cole:** 27; **Richard Bruhn:** 67; **Shane and Tammy Bryant:** 79, 80; **Ray Buckner:** 24; **Jerry and Carol Buczkowski:** 65; **Jim Buhle:** 79; **Bret Byus:** 18; **Tom Cahill:** 136; **Rick Cain:** 38; **Gary Campbell:** 136; **Rick Campbell:** 71; **Tim Carie:** 72; **James H. Carson:** 138; **Greg and Cecilia Carter:** 29; **June Cecil:** 125; **Luis A. Chanes:** 71; **Tom Chinn:** 19, 30, 113, 128, 133, 134; **Peter Ciccone:** 45; **Tom Clary:** 121; **Bill Clemens:** 114; **John Cook:** 72; **Ray Cordrey:** 26, 41; **Robert and Karen Courtway:** 81; **Ed Cunneen:** 120; **Rick Cybul:** 133; **Terry D. Davis:** 60; **Mason Dixon:** 23; **Greg Don:** 131; **Richard Douglas:** 35; **Bill Draper:** 73; **Duffy's Collectible Cars:** 119; **Tim Dusek:** 32; **Richard Ellis:** 75; **James and Mary Engle:** 113; **Phil Fair:** 14; **Scott Field:** 146; **Stan Fritzinger:** 36; **David M. Gabay:** 33; **Gil Garcia:** 18; **Tony Garcia:** 108; **Larry Gordon:** 108; **John Gricki Jr.:** 39; **Gary Grillo:** 135; **Otto Groth:** 38; **Siegfried Grunze:** 79; **Mike Guarise:** 129; **Denny Guest:** 15; **Henry Hart:** 109; **Wayne Hartye:** 31; **Bill Hoff:** 146; **Roger Holdaway:** 67; **Clarence Hudinski:** 27; **Derek K. Humphrey:** 73; **Jeff Hyosaka:** 121; **E. J. and Rachelle Jaymeson:** 141; **Albert A. Jones:** 111; **Chris and Greg Joseph:** 121; **Tony Kanzia:** 85; **Douglas Keller:** 146; **Charles M. Kerr:** 137; **Mark Knecht:**

120; **Fred and Chris Kuebler:** 128; **Jim Labertew:** 19; **Richard Ladd:** 76; **Brian Lang:** 28; **Tom Lembeck:** 37; **Michael Leone Sr.:** 23; **Ken Lingenfelter:** 91; **Dave Lingle:** 34; **Douglas Lombardo:** 64; **Rob Lynch:** 122; **Bob Macy:** 130; **Larry Maisel:** 62, 63; **Phillip Manoanici:** 137; **Browney L. Mascow:** 26; **Steve Maysonet:** 119; **Brian R. McArthur:** 118; **Larry and Karen Miller:** 130; **Amos Minter:** 15; **Randy Mitchell:** 126; **Ray Morrison:** 117; **Bob Mosher:** 14, 15, 16; **Ronald S. Mroz:** 115, 116; **Randy Mucha:** 137; **Kenneth R. Mullany:** 76; **MyHotCars.com:** 121; **Kenneth Nagel:** 69, 122; **Matt Neale:** 17; **Terry Nelson:** 68; **Phil Newcomb:** 38; **Northwest Auto Sales/Rick Robinson:** 117, 122, 131; **John R. Oehler:** 130, 138, 140; **D. R. Ogsberger:** 117; **Norm Olsen:** 20; **Mike Patak:** 63; **Randy Paxton:** 45; **Leon Perahia:** 39; **Jeff Peterson:** 27; **Donald Phillips:** 30; **Wayne Piper:** 40; **Chris Piscitello:** 113; **Charles Plylar:** 68; **Steve Potsek:** 75; **Pat Price:** 64; **John Prokop:** 74; **Larry Raines:** 72; **Mike Riefer:** 35; **RK Motors Charlotte:** back cover, 18, 116, 120, 123, 141; **Keith Rohm:** 23; **Tom Runge:** 75; **Jeff Ruppert:** 127; **Steve Sadler:** 32; **Richard and Betty Sarallo:** 29; **Joe L. Saunders:** 19; **Brian L. Sbardelli:** 81; **Tom Schlitter:** 70; **Daniel Schmitt and Co.:** 66; **Gary Schneider:** 22; **Bill Schultz:** 124; **Dean Skinner:** 115; **John Skwirblies:** 135; **Gary D. Smith:** 112; **Southwest Gallery of Cars:** 77; **Candy and Tom Spiel:** 118; **Frank Spittle:** 112; **SS Classics/Steve Schultz:** 109, 115, 117, 120; **Nathan Struder:** 18; **Jim and Stacy Swarbrick:** 129; **Brian Thomason:** 110; **Jason Thompson:** 71; **Barry Troup:** 112; **Dennis A. Urban:** 110; **Volo Auto Museum:** 25; **Doug Vura:** 41; **Mark and Joni Walters:** 139; **Larry Webb:** 141; **Tom Weed:** 134; **George Weisser:** 42; **Bob Wells:** 61; **John Wells:** 34; **Odus West:** 35; **Leroy and Judy Williams:** 136; **Judy Williamson:** 41; **Walter P. Wise:** 74; **Aaron Yurkanin:** 45; **Dominic Zambuto:** 43; **Frank Zilka:** 17

Future car concept/illustrations by Thom Taylor

Our appreciation to the historical archives and media services groups at Chrysler Group LLC, Ford Motor Company, and General Motors Company.

About the Editors of Consumer Guide®:

For more than 40 years, Consumer Guide® has been a trusted provider of new-car buying information.

The Consumer Guide® staff drives and evaluates more than 200 vehicles annually.

Consumerguide.com is one of the Web's most popular automotive resources, visited by more than two million shoppers monthly.

The Editors of Consumer Guide® also publish the award-winning bimonthly *Collectible Automobile*® magazine.

CONTENTS

FOREWORD

I t's commonly held knowledge that the 1964-71 period was the golden age of the muscle car. The 1964 Pontiac GTO set the blueprint, other manufacturers jumped on the bandwagon, and by 1970, the craze had reached its pinnacle. It was a high-performance wonderland: Magnum 500s and rally wheels on white-letter wide-oval tires. Eye-searing colors with wacky names such as Orbit Orange, Grabber Green, and Plum Crazy. Wild stripes and bulging hoods with functional scoops. And, of course, unbelievably brawny big-block power.

And, just like that, the original muscle-car era passed . . . almost as quickly as it arrived. It's in the past, and it can never be fully recaptured.

Now, let's jump to the present. Though the glory days of the first muscle-car era are gone forever, they left an indelible imprint on automotive history. The breed never died out completely, and a strong case can be made that a second muscle-car golden age is at its peak now. The Chevrolet Camaro and Dodge Challenger are back . . . and the Ford Mustang never went away. All three are stronger than ever. Legendary names live again: SS, ZL1, R/T, Hemi, Super Bee, Boss 302, GT500. It's a wonderland all over again.

What's more, almost 50 years of ever-improving automotive technology has enabled today's muscle cars to reach breathtaking new heights of performance and refinement. There was a time not so long ago when it seemed certain that the 450-hp rating of the 1970 Chevelle SS 454 would never be equaled. Today, the top versions of all three Detroit ponycars surpass it, even with the more-stringent emissions controls and more-realistic horsepower-rating standards of today. In fact, the soon-to-arrive 2013 Shelby GT500 Mustang beats it by 212 horsepower. Unbelievable.

As this book is written, the current Camaro, Challenger, and Mustang are all at or near a crossroads. The Camaro and Mustang are both set to be redesigned within the next couple years, and at this point it seems likely that the Challenger may be retired in favor of a revived Barracuda.

What does the future hold? Will the 2013 Shelby GT500 remain the benchmark? Will the next generation of Detroit's muscular ponycars raise the performance bar even higher, or will there be a retreat from extreme horsepower like there was in the early 1970s?

The answers will come soon enough. For now, *Muscle Cars: Past Present Future* chronicles and celebrates these fascinating machines.

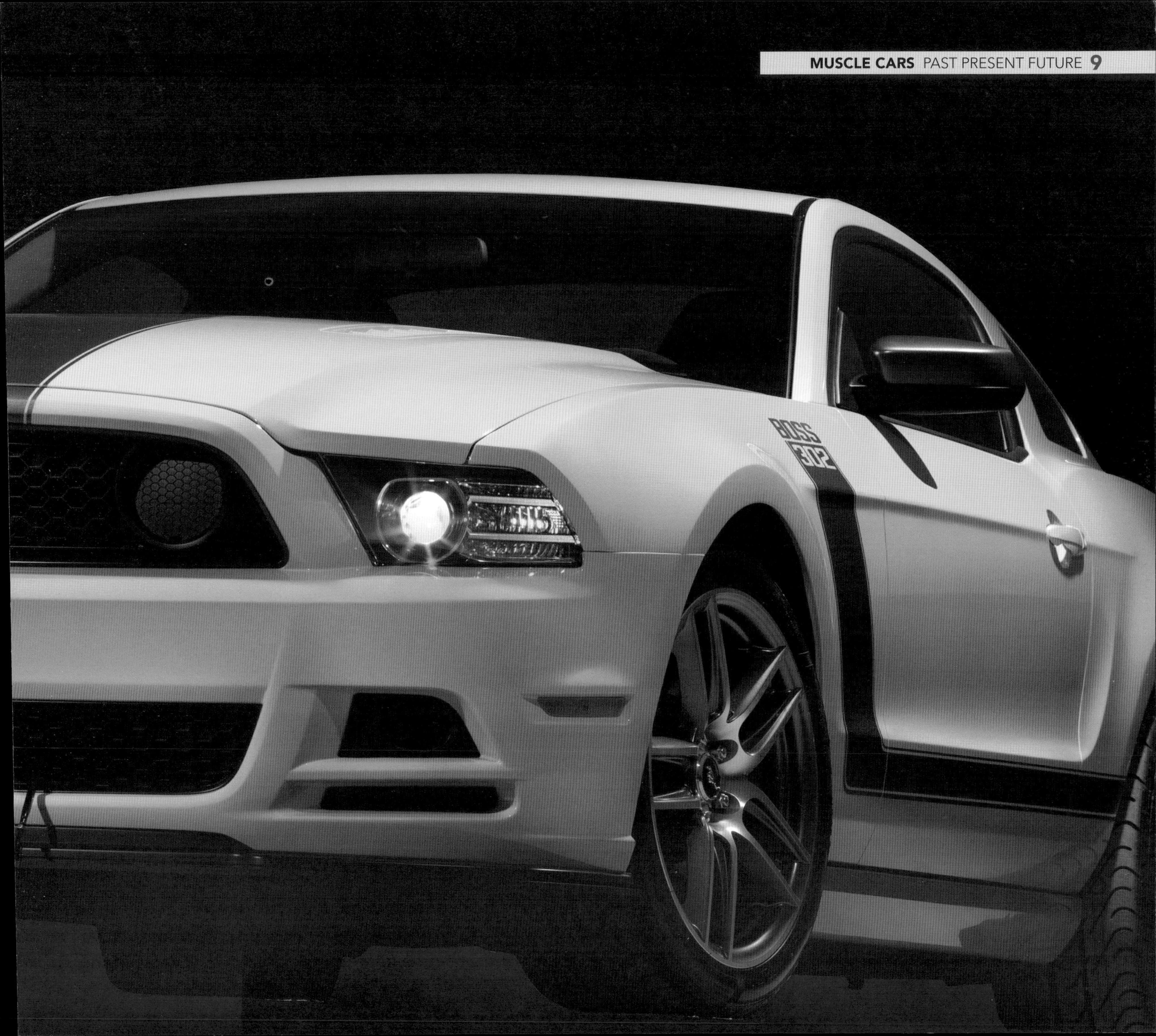
BOSS
302

'cuda 440·6

CHRYSLER CORPORATION

To properly trace the lineage of Mopar muscle, the best place to start is at the dawn of the "horsepower race" of the 1950s. Chrysler Corporation didn't have the first modern short-stroke/overhead-valve V-8 engine, but the company's initial effort was a really good one. Chrysler's FirePower Hemi of 1951 displaced the same 331 cubic inches as Cadillac's V-8, but made 180 horsepower compared to 160 in the Caddy.

The power advantage was attributable to an efficient hemispherical combustion chamber that was able to use more of the heat energy in the burning fuel than other designs. This allowed a Hemi to run at lower compression than other engines, and also allowed the use of regular-grade gasoline rather than more-expensive premium fuel. The FirePower engine also offered tremendous opportunities to increase horsepower with relatively minor modifications. The main problem with the design was the complexity of the valvetrain, which made the Hemi expensive to produce.

DeSoto added a smaller FireDome Hemi in 1952, and Dodge a smaller-still Red Ram version in 1953. Then, for 1955, Chrysler introduced the C-300 two-door hardtop with a 300-horsepower 331. This was 50 more horsepower than the New Yorker, and marked the start of the 300 "Letter" series. By 1957's 300C, the Hemi had grown to 392 cubic inches and was putting out 375 horsepower.

The 1959 300E lost the Hemi, but had a new 413-cubic-inch "Wedge" V-8 and 380 horses. The Hemi was a fine engine, but its high production costs led Chrysler to focus on the more-economical-to-build Wedge engine. The Wedge went on to form the basis for most of Mopar's high-performance mills of the 1960s and '70s—by 1960, Plymouth cataloged a 330-horsepower 383, and Dodge had a 340-horse version of the same engine.

A false rumor that Chevrolet was going to make their 1962 models smaller directly led to downsized (and curiously styled) '62 Dodges and Plymouths that never caught on with mainstream buyers. However, the sensible dimensions and lower weight of these cars, combined with the potent "Max Wedge" 410-hp 413 V-8, made them very popular and competitive at the drag strip.

For '63, the quirky styling was cleaned up, and the hottest engines displaced 426 cubic inches and made as much as 425 horsepower. These Max Wedge motors were serious contenders in the Super Stock drag wars of the early Sixties, and Dodge was quick to brag about the exploits of its factory-backed Ramchargers racing team in advertisements.

The 426 Max Wedges returned for 1964, but at the Daytona 500 in February, Chrysler introduced a new engine destined for legendary status: the 426 Hemi. The name again came from the engine's hemispherical combustion chambers, similar to the design Chrysler used in the Fifties. A race-only engine in '64, the 426 Hemi came in NASCAR and drag versions. The engine dominated that year's Daytona 500, with Richard Petty in the #43 Plymouth easily winning a lopsided race. Petty went on to win the season championship. Hemis performed equally well on the strip, and their race-only status carried into 1965.

The hottest Mopar street cars in 1964 and '65 were powered by a 426 "Street Wedge" with a single four-barrel carb and 365 horsepower. On the racing front, the Hemi fell afoul of NASCAR rule makers for 1965. As a result, Dodge and Plymouth ended up sitting out the first part of the season. Ford dominated in their absence, winning 48 of 55 races.

In the meantime, Mopar drag-racing efforts reached new heights with a small run of factory-built altered-wheelbase (AWB) Hemi-powered Dodge Coronets and Plymouth Belvederes. The AWB cars had the front and rear wheels dramatically shifted forward to improve weight distribution and weight transfer, which greatly increased traction at the drag strip. These radically altered production cars had a bizarre appearance that prompted the name "funny car."

Big news came for 1966: The new intermediate-size Plymouths and Dodges (including the flashy, fastback-bodied Charger) were offered with an optional "Street Hemi." Though detuned from the race motors, the 426 Hemi was still rated at a formidable 425 horsepower. However, the Hemi remained very expensive, adding about $1000 to the price of a car so equipped. Also, Hemi-powered cars didn't look much different from their less-muscular brethren, lacking visual doodads like the add-on scoops and stripes that were beginning to define the fast evolving "muscle car."

Appearance was addressed in 1967, when dedicated Mopar performance models arrived in showrooms. The Dodge Coronet R/T and Plymouth GTX had put all the expected muscle-car pieces together in a single, easy-to-identify package. The pair also introduced a less-expensive performance engine, the 440. On the street, it was nearly as fierce as the optional Hemi, but a 440 was easier to maintain, and its lower price put serious muscle within reach of a larger audience.

Taking that concept further, Plymouth pioneered the low-budget muscle car with the 1968 Road Runner, a bare-bones Belvedere pillared coupe with a hopped-up version of Chrysler's faithful 383-cubic-inch engine. Fitted with several parts from the 440, the Road Runner engine put out 335 horsepower. The mighty Hemi was the only optional mill. Prices started at a frugal $2896, versus $3355 for a GTX. Plymouth predicted around 2500 Road Runner sales for '68; the actual number was 44,599.

Dodge quickly cooked up a similar budget muscle car of its own, the 1968 Coronet Super Bee. A breathtaking new Charger appeared for 1968 too, and a bevy of Mopar's mightiest engines were available in the R/T version. Unfortunately, the new Charger's NASCAR superspeedway performance didn't match its racy styling, so Dodge added a slicked-up, more-aerodynamic Charger 500 in '69. After it fell short of Ford's finest on the track, Mopar engineers pulled out the stops and created a pointy-nose, high-wing version, the Charger Daytona. Street versions were tough to miss.

Plymouth's 1970 Superbird applied the Daytona playbook to the Road Runner, and arguably its biggest win was in helping lure Richard Petty back to the Plymouth camp. (Petty had defected to archrival Ford for the '69 season, angry that Plymouth didn't have an equivalent to the swoopy Dodge Chargers.)

The muscle-car era peaked in 1970, just in time for Chrysler's all-new ponycars: the Dodge Challenger and Plymouth 'Cuda. With their knockout long-hood/short-deck styling, sinister stance, and huge list of "with-it" options, these new "E-Body" Mopars were arguably the most attractive and desirable muscle cars Chrysler ever built. Every performance engine in the corporate arsenal was available: 340, 383, 440 Magnum, 440 six-barrel, and 426 Hemi. A full palette of bright colors and a wide array of stripes, scoops, and spoilers allowed for unprecedented personalization right on the factory floor.

Compact performance cars had been around for a few years, one of Chrysler's earliest being the 1965 Plymouth

Barracuda Formula S with its 273-cubic-inch, 235-horsepower, solid-lifter V-8. For 1970, Plymouth built an attractive Duster off humble, low-cost Valiant mechanicals, similar to the way the original Barracuda was created. With Mopar's high-revving 340, the Duster 340 offered excellent acceleration at low cost. The next year, Dodge added its Demon version (which was later renamed Dart Sport), and the pair carried the compact-performance banner through the mid-Seventies.

The 426 Hemi hung on through 1971, but Detroit performance was already fading fast. Challenger and Barracuda were dropped after '74, following four years of declining sales. By '75, Road Runner was demoted to an appearance package for the Fury, and Charger had evolved into a luxury-themed coupe. The Road Runner and R/T nameplates shifted to the new Plymouth Volaré and Dodge Aspen compacts in 1976, but these cars were solidly in the "tape-stripe muscle" camp; they offered flashy looks, but not the performance to back it up. By 1980, rear-drive muscle was gone from Chrysler.

From the 1980s to the early 2000s, rear-drive V-8 passenger cars were in hibernation at Chrysler, and Mopar performance took the shape of turbocharged four-cylinder engines in front-drive cars. Carroll Shelby was even enlisted to help burnish Dodge's street cred with various hot-rodded K-car derivatives. These hot compacts didn't fit the definition of a "true" traditional muscle car, but they did help keep Mopar performance alive.

Chrysler's performance reputation was supercharged overnight with the 1989 introduction of the show-stealing Dodge Viper RT/10 concept. This raw, breathtaking, two-seat roadster boldly revived the spirit of the hallowed Sixties Shelby Cobra 427SC. Enthusiasts begged Dodge to build it, and Dodge complied—following a whirlwind development cycle, production Vipers were ready for the 1992 model year. Power came from a 400-horsepower 8.2-liter V-10 adapted from a Dodge truck engine. It wasn't a traditional muscle car either, but the Viper made it clear that unfettered Detroit performance was still possible.

As the new millennium dawned, the Plymouth brand was on its last legs, and was relegated to history in mid-2001, after a final Neon compact was built. Mopar fans mourned the loss, but they had something to cheer about when a new generation of Hemi V-8s was introduced just a couple years

later. The new Hemi, a state-of-the-art 5.7-liter V-8 with 345 horsepower, bowed in mid-2003 as an option in the Dodge Ram pickup truck. It migrated to passenger cars for 2005, when the full-size, rear-wheel-drive Chrysler 300C sedan and Dodge Magnum RT wagon debuted. The base 300C and Magnum RT were plenty gutsy, but even more power was just around the corner. High-performance SRT8 (Street and Racing Technology) versions of the 300C and Magnum followed, both with a 425-horsepower 6.1-liter version of the new Hemi.

Meanwhile, Dodge began digging into its rich muscle-car heritage for its new models. For 2006, Dodge revived the Charger name on a rakish new four-door sedan based on the 300/Magnum chassis. (Some Mopar traditionalists were rankled by the fact that the new Charger was not a two-door coupe, but most seemed to get over it quickly.) Shortly thereafter, the success of Ford's retro-look 2005 Mustang spurred Dodge to bring back its iconic Challenger. At the 2006 Detroit Auto Show, Dodge pulled the wraps off the Challenger Concept, a new-millennium reimagining of the classic 1970 original based on a shortened Charger chassis. It was in production by 2008.

Chrysler came perilously close to going out of business when the worst recession since the 1930s swept around the globe in late 2008. Bankruptcy followed in 2009, with financing from the U.S. and Canadian governments the only saving grace. As part of the painful process, management control was transferred to Italian automaker Fiat.

Despite scarce product-development funds, Dodge managed to keep the Charger and Challenger fresh in the eyes of the car-buying public by trading on the heritage of the 1968-71 "golden-age" of Mopar muscle. A parade of new "High Impact" paint hues, cartoon Super Bees, R/T stripes, flat-black accents, hood scoops, and spoilers kept these cars exciting in Chrysler's trying times.

And, once on steady ground again with Fiat, Chrysler seemed to step up the pace. The Challenger SRT8 picked up a new 6.4-liter Hemi for 2011; not only did horsepower increase to 470, the engine displaced 392 cubic inches just like the big Hemis of the late Fifties. Charger and 300 were redesigned for 2011, and the new SRT8 variants that appeared for 2012 used the menacing 6.4 Hemi too. Even with a new hand at the tiller, Mopar muscle seems as strong as ever.

► *1962 DODGE*

DART

A Chrysler executive heard talk at a party that Chevrolet was going to make the brand's full-size cars smaller for 1962. It wasn't true, but Chrysler management's overreaction to the "news" resulted in shrunken 1962 Dodge and Plymouth models. The new size and love-it-or-leave-it styling made for sales disasters. Darts were Dodge's stripper models in 1962, but when equipped with the available 410-horsepower "Ramcharger" 413-cid V-8, they were drag-strip terrors. The Ramcharger was intended for "sanctioned acceleration trials," not for the street.

◄ *1962 PLYMOUTH*

BELVEDERE

Like Dodge, Plymouth struggled in 1962 with controversial styling. Seven inches shorter, and up to 400 pounds lighter than a '61 model, the new cars were seriously fast with the 410-hp 413. Plymouth dubbed its version of this wedge-head engine the Super Stock 413, no doubt in honor of the Super Stock classes these Mopars, like this bare-bones Belvedere two-door sedan, soon ruled at the nation's drag strips. The engine was also known by the unofficial "Max Wedge" title.

► *1962 PLYMOUTH*

BELVEDERE

Plymouth power and low weight paid off in a historic quarter-mile run by Tom Grove in July 1962. Grove's Super Stock Belvedere ran the quarter in 11.93 seconds at 118.57 mph. His was the first stock passenger automobile to beat 12 seconds in the quarter mile. Here, Grove is behind the wheel of his "Melrose Missile II" at the '62 Winternationals.

◀ *1963 DODGE*
330

For 1963, the Ramcharger 413 was bored out to 426 cubic inches. It made 415 horsepower on 11.0:1 compression, or 425 on 13.5:1. This bare-bones 330 two-door sedan has a close-ratio three-speed manual transmission with floor shift, but a heavy-duty pushbutton TorqueFlite automatic was also available.

▶ *1963 DODGE*
POLARA 500

Sagging '62 sales taught Dodge its lesson. Styling for '63 was redone, and the cleaner lines were handsome. Wheelbases were up three inches, to 119. Dodges were available in 330, 440, Polara, and Polara 500 trim (shown). Polara 500s wore prominent color sweep side trim, bright sill and wheel-lip moldings, a ribbed quarter-panel piece that visually extended the rear-bumper wraparound, and a bright molding at the base of the C-pillar. Of course, the hot 426 engine was available too.

▶ *1963 PLYMOUTH*
BELVEDERE

Plymouths wore cleaned up styling for 1963 as well, but retained the 116-inch wheelbase used on the '62s. They gained the new Super Stock 426 engines, in the same horsepower ratings the Dodges had. Street versions were available through any dealer, but these engines were really only suited to the track. Tom Grove remained one of the West Coast's quickest Mopar drag racers.

▶ *1964 DODGE & PLYMOUTH*

426 HEMI

Dodge (left) and Plymouth (right) models wore handsome styling in 1964. In February, Chrysler unleashed a new Hemi V-8 at Daytona. Based on the 426 wedge, the new Hemi had heads with half-arc combustion chambers that allowed fuel to burn quicker and more completely. The engine breathed better thanks to the head's complex valve network with dual rocker shafts. Still displacing 426 cubic inches, the "race" Hemi quickly swept the first three spots in the Daytona 500, with Richard Petty winning in a Plymouth. NASCAR versions of the engine used a single four-barrel carb, while drag versions used dual quads. Horsepower was rated at a maximum 425, but a Hemi was actually making around 570. Street versions of the 426 Hemi were still a couple years away.

▶ *1965 DODGE*

CORONET A990

Dodge made a limited run of drag-race-ready 1965 Coronet two-door sedans under the order code A990. All were equipped with the 426 "Hemi-Charger" engine under the scooped hood. Weight was saved through the use of thinner sheetmetal and lightweight interior trim. Even the normal Coronet four-headlamp setup was reduced to a pair. The $4717 cars were sold as-is with no warranty. By comparison, a base Coronet two-door sedan with the 273-cid V-8 stickered for $2313. Just 101 A990 Coronets were built; this is one of six with a manual transmission.

▲ *1964 DODGE*

426 WEDGE

Dodge and Plymouth still offered hot 426 wedge engines in 1964 as well. The 415- and 425-horse variants used dual four-barrel carbs and unusual upswept headers that allowed the engine to breathe freely but still fit into the car's narrow engine bay. An easier-to-manage "Street Wedge" variant with a single four-barrel and 365 horsepower debuted too. It had a chrome air cleaner and valve covers, but made do with regular exhaust manifolds rather than headers.

▼ *1965 PLYMOUTH*
BELVEDERE I A990

Plymouth's version of the A990 drag car was based on the Belvedere I and listed for $4671. Just like in the Dodge, the Hemi engine—called Super Commando by Plymouth's marketing department—was modestly rated at 425 horsepower. Torque was 480 pound-feet. The engines were hand assembled by select technicians at Chrysler's Marine and Industrial Division plant in Marysville, Michigan. Chrysler warned prospective customers to expect a rough idle, high oil consumption, poor gas mileage, and objectionable engine noise. Plymouth A990 production totaled 102. Only a dozen had the four-speed manual transmission with floor shift; the balance ran a heavy-duty TorqueFlite automatic.

▲ *1965 PLYMOUTH*
BARRACUDA FORMULA S

Sporty compacts were increasingly popular, and Plymouth's Barracuda bowed during 1964. Based on the Valiant, the bubble-back Barracuda was the best-selling Plymouth by 1965. The Formula S package added a little muscle in the form of a 235-horsepower, 273-cubic-inch "Commando" V-8. Other goodies included heavy-duty suspension, fatter Goodyear Blue Streak tires on 14-inch wheels, and a 6000-rpm tach. *Car and Driver* did 0-60 mph in 9.1 seconds and the quarter in 17.5 at 88.5 mph. *Hot Rod* turned a 16.43 at 89.

▶ *1966 DODGE*
CORONET 440

Nineteen Sixty-Six was the year of the Street Hemi. At Dodge, the new detuned version of the '65 race engine was available in the restyled Coronet and the new Charger. Still rated at 425 horsepower, the 426-cubic-inch engine added about $1000 to the $2551 base price of the Coronet 440 hardtop. Hemi cars received stiffer springs and bigger (11-inch) brakes. Front discs were optional. The result was big-league quick. *Car and Driver*'s test car did 0-60 mph in 5.3 seconds and the quarter in 13.8 at 104 mph. *Motor Trend* called the acceleration "Absolutely shattering."

▲ 1966 DODGE
CHARGER

Charger bowed for 1966 based heavily on the 117-inch-wheelbase Coronet. Though the two shared much, Charger's racy fastback roofline, hidden headlamps, and full-width taillights made for dramatically different styling. Charger also had a state-of-the-art '60s interior with lots of chrome, four bucket seats, available center consoles front and rear, and full instrumentation including a 150-mph speedometer and a 6000-rpm tach. At $3122 to start, Charger priced $417 more than a top-line Coronet 500 hardtop. Of 37,344 first-year Chargers built, a mere 468 had the Street Hemi.

▲ 1967 DODGE
CORONET R/T

Coronet changed little for '67, but Dodge did add the R/T—for "Road and Track"—as the new muscle model. Standard were fake hood vents, a Charger-inspired grille with exposed head-lamps, and the biggest displacement V-8 of the day, Mopar's 440. At 375 horsepower, the 440 Magnum was more flexible, easier to maintain, and cheaper than a Hemi. It also had nearly as much torque and at lower RPM. Properly tuned, a 440 could stay with the Hemi up to 70-80 mph. *Hot Rod's* test 440 with TorqueFlite ran the quarter in 14.91 seconds at 93.16 mph. The Hemi was the lone engine option for the R/T, but only 283 were ordered.

▼ 1966 PLYMOUTH
SATELLITE

At Plymouth, the intermediate Belvedere series was completely redesigned for '66. The top-line Belvedere hardtop and convertible were called Satellite. Restrained exterior bright work, a stylish bucket seat interior, and full wheel covers with simulated knock-offs really dressed up the Satellite. The 425-horsepower Street Hemi was the top engine option for Belvederes. Only 503 Satellite hardtops had the Hemi and a four-speed manual transmission. Another 314 carried the Hemi backed by TorqueFlite.

▼ 1967 PLYMOUTH
BARRACUDA FORMULA S

The second-generation Barracuda appeared as a 1967 model. A fastback model returned, and hardtop and convertible body styles were added. Enthusiasts could choose between one of two Formula S packages, each with upgraded suspension and Firestone redline tires. One Formula S package brought a small-block 273-cubic-inch V-8, good for 235 horsepower. The other delivered Chrysler's 383-cube big-block V-8 rated at 280 ponies (below). The big engine was a tight squeeze in the Barracuda, so air conditioning and power steering weren't available, simply because the components wouldn't fit.

▼ *1967 PLYMOUTH*
GTX

Plymouth added a muscle variant of the Belvedere/Satellite for 1967, the GTX. It came in hardtop and convertible styles, all with snazzy bucket-seat interiors and a 375-horsepower 440. The Street Hemi was the only optional engine. Dual nonfunctional hood scoops and a flip-open gas cap added some visual punch to the exterior, as did optional racing stripes for the hood and deck. The hardtop priced from $3178, the convertible $3418. GTX production totaled 12,010 cars, only 680 of them convertibles.

▲ *1968 DODGE*
DART GTS

Dodge added a big-block 383-powered Dart GTS model late in the 1967 model year. The facelifted '68s had GTSes as a regular part of the lineup. Standard power switched to a new 275-horsepower, 340-cubic-inch V-8. A 300-horse 383 was optional. *Car and Driver* was smitten with the 340: "The latest word from the underground is that the little Mopar 340 is the hot set-up. A giant killer from Hamtramck . . . easily the most exciting engine Chrysler has produced since the Hemi . . . We're believers." The magazine reported a 0–60 mph time of six seconds flat, and the quarter in 14.4 at 99 mph.

▼ *1968 DODGE*
DART HEMI

On March 4, 1968, Dodge began offering racers purpose-built Dart drag machines equipped with the mighty 426 Hemi. These were no street cars; the package included fiberglass fenders and hood, a huge hood scoop, acid-dipped body, plexiglass windows, and lightweight seats from Dodge's A-100 van with trick drilled-aluminum frames. The rear wheel wells were opened up for big slicks, and the car's battery was relocated to the trunk. Just 80 were built.

▲ *1968 DODGE*
CORONET SUPER BEE

Super Bee was a midyear addition to the 1968 Coronet line. Less expensive than a Coronet R/T, Super Bee was Dodge's response to Plymouth's popular, budget-friendly Road Runner. Super Bee's $3037 base price included a 335-horse 383, four-speed with Hurst shifter, heavy-duty suspension, and Charger instrumentation. The Hemi was optional. A pillared coupe was the only Super Bee body style for '68.

▲ 1968 DODGE
CORONET R/T

Like other '68 Coronets, the R/T wrapped new sheetmetal around its carryover platform. Mopar's fine 375-horse 440-cube Magnum V-8 was standard. The Hemi was optional, but only 230 buyers checked that box. *Motor Trend*'s 440 TorqueFlite test car went 0-60 mph in 6.9 seconds and ran the quarter in 15.1 seconds at 95 mph.

'68 DODGE CHARGER R/T

Run with the Dodge Scat Pack

▲ 1968 DODGE
CHARGER R/T

Tongue-in-cheek icons and wild graphics were part of late-'60s culture, and Dodge was right there with the "Scat Pack" bumblebee. Charter members of Dodge's "Scat Pack" performance team for '68 were the Dart GTS, Coronet R/T, and Charger R/T. Audiences of the hit film *Bullitt* thrilled as the new 440 Magnum-equipped Charger R/T tore about hilly San Francisco in a classic duel with Steve McQueen's 390 Mustang. Would McQueen have caught a Hemi?

1968 DODGE
CHARGER R/T HEMI

The second-generation Charger was one of the '60s' handsomest muscle cars, aptly described by *Car and Driver* as "all guts and purpose." At $3480, the R/T included the 440 Magnum, heavy-duty brakes, R/T handling package, and F70×14 Red Streak or white sidewall tires. A full-width hidden-headlamp grille, flying buttress rear roof, and race-inspired fender-top gas cap were Charger trademarks. Production increased to 96,100, but only 475 were ordered with the Hemi. With TorqueFlite and standard 3.23:1 gears, *Car and Driver*'s Hemi Charger got to 60 mph in six seconds and turned a killer 13.5 at 105 in the quarter.

◀ *1968 PLYMOUTH*

BARRACUDA

Rarest of the '68 Barracudas were the relative handful (perhaps only 75 at most) of fastbacks fitted with the 426 Hemi for drag racing. Finished by Hurst Performance, the cars had a fiberglass hood and fenders, lightweight doors, and a stripped interior using Dodge A-100 van seats and plastic windows. The competition-only cars weighed in around 3000 pounds, significantly lighter than a stock Barracuda. The race Hemi engine came with dual quads on a cross-ram intake, competition headers, and race exhaust. Four-speed manual or TorqueFlite automatic transmissions were available. Here, "Mr. Four-Speed" Ronnie Sox poses with the Sox & Martin Hemi Barracuda.

1968 PLYMOUTH

ROAD RUNNER

Muscle cars quickly evolved from mainstream models with expensive special engines to expensive special models with expensive special engines. What the youth of America needed was an inexpensive special model with an inexpensive special engine. In 1968, Plymouth gave it to them in the form of the Road Runner. It started with the lightest, least expensive Belvedere pillared coupe. Under the hood was Mopar's 383, but fitted with several go-fast pieces from the big, bad 440. With a single four-barrel, the new mill made 335 horsepower.

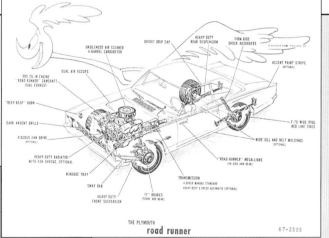

1968 PLYMOUTH
ROAD RUNNER HEMI

Plymouth paid Warner Bros. $50,000 for the rights to decorate their new muscle model with the name and likeness of the famous speedy cartoon bird. It was exactly the right touch. Priced from a stingy $2896, the Road Runner was a smash hit. Plymouth thought 2500 would be sold; buyers snapped up nearly 45,000 in the first year. Serious-minded standard features included a strengthened four-speed manual, 3.23:1 rear gears, beefed-up suspension, heavy-duty drum brakes, and Polyglas F70×14 tires. The 383's 15-second quarter-mile times were a bit disappointing, but an $88 High-Performance Axle package with 3.55:1 cogs wrung a bit more from the 383. But low-13s were just $714 away via the lone engine option: a 425-horse 426 Hemi.

◄ 1968 PLYMOUTH
GTX

With the hot new Road Runner anchoring the lower rungs, the familiar GTX returned to top off Plymouth's mid-size muscle ladder. In keeping with its upscale mission, the GTX came in two-door hardtop and convertible body styles. The 375-horsepower 440 remained standard, with the take-no-prisoners Hemi the sole engine option. The TorqueFlite automatic transmission was standard, with four-speed manual a no-cost alternative. While even a loaded Road Runner was plain, the GTX dressed its part with extra bright trim and double side stripes. A hood with nonfunctional vents was common to both cars. Inside, the well-appointed Sport Satellite interior with shiny details and fake woodgrain replaced the Road Runner's fleet-grade trim. The differences showed in base prices: $3355 for the GTX hardtop, $3034 for the Road Runner coupe. This year's GTX production was 17,500, including 450 with the Hemi.

▶ *1969 DODGE*

DART SWINGER 340

If Dodge had an engine to rival the energetic small-block Chevy, it was the eager, free-revving 340-cubic-inch V-8. Taking a cue from the low-buck success of the Super Bee and Plymouth Road Runner, Dodge added a new budget performance model to the '69 Dart lineup: the Swinger 340. Equipment included the 275-horse 340, four-speed with Hurst shifter, heavy-duty suspension, dual exhausts, bulged hood with die-cast louvers, and the Scat Pack's trademark "bumblebee" stripes. Interior trim was simple to help keep the price to a reasonable $2836. A hardtop coupe was the only body style.

▲ *1969 DODGE*

DART GTS

The showcase performance Dart GTS remained available in '69 too. As with the Swinger 340, the 275-horse 340 was standard. The GTS body had more bright trim though, and the interior was much nicer. Expected performance cues were present, including a louvered hood, GTS emblems, and bumblebee stripe. The hardtop started at $3226, the convertible from $3419. Underrated at 275 horsepower, a 340 Dart could crack off easy mid-14-second quarter-mile ETs, to the embarrassment of many a big-block supercar. But this was the 1960s. Balance and finesse were not the order of the day.

▼ *1969 DODGE*

DART GTS

If the 340 was good, a 383-cube Dart would be even better. Right? Not necessarily, as it turned out. The 383 four-barrel was optional in Dart GTS. It was rated at a realistic 300 horses. The 340, however, actually produced 300 ponies or more, and weighed 90 pounds less than the big-block 383. Where the 340 was a fine match for the GTS's heavy-duty suspension, allowing power to flow smoothly to the pavement, the 383 upset this balance. Traction off the line was poor, and ETs were no quicker. The big-block wasn't the best all-around engine in a Dart, but what would the '60s have been without a little excess?

1969 DODGE
SUPER BEE 440 SIX PACK

In mid-1969, Chrysler engineers used some good ol' hot-rodding savvy to create one of the muscle era's most intoxicating cars. They took Mopar's fine 375-horse 440 Magnum and treated it to the time-honored hop-up of more carburetion, replacing the single Carter quad with three Holley two-barrels on an Edelbrock Hi-Riser manifold. Hemi valve springs, a hotter cam, magnafluxed connecting rods, and other fortifications helped boost horsepower to 390. A Hurst-shifted four-speed and 4.10:1 rear were standard. TorqueFlite was optional, but disc brakes and air conditioning were not allowed. The 440 Six Pack package added $463 to the cost of a Super Bee—about $400 less than a Hemi. Included were plain steel wheels adorned only by chrome lug nuts and a wild lift-off fiberglass hood.

▶ 1969 DODGE
CORONET R/T

Coronet R/T returned for '69 with a revised grille and taillamps, but few other alterations. The 375-horse 440 Magnum continued as standard; the 425-horse 426 Hemi was optional. A new option for 383 Super Bees and 440 Coronet R/Ts, and standard on Hemi R/Ts, was a Ramcharger fresh-air induction package with a two-scoop hood. R/Ts could also be ordered with the "Track Pack." The R/T hardtop started at $3442, and the convertible at $3660.

▼ 1969 DODGE
CHARGER R/T

Charger R/Ts didn't change much for 1969. The grille picked up a louvered divider; elongated taillamps replaced four round ones; and the bucket seats were revised. Dodge built 20,057 Charger R/Ts for 1969. The majority had the standard 375-horsepower four-barrel 440 Magnum. Just 232 were ordered with the 426 Hemi, which again was the only R/T engine option.

▲ 1969 DODGE
CHARGER 500

"Win on Sunday, Sell on Monday" was a Detroit mantra in the 1960s. It was truest of NASCAR performance, and the war between Chrysler and Ford for superspeedway supremacy produced some of the most outlandish cars of the muscle age. Dodge's '68 Charger was an aerodynamic washout on 190-mph high-bank ovals. To reduce drag, Mopar engineers plugged the nose cavity with a flush-mounted Coronet grille. At the rear, lift was quelled by replacing the recessed "flying buttress" backlight with a flush-mounted rear window. The new racer was called Charger 500, and 392 similarly modified production cars were built to qualify it for NASCAR.

▲ 1969 DODGE
CHARGER DAYTONA

Racing Charger 500s captured 18 victories in '69. Trouble was, Ford's droop-nosed aero warriors won 30. Mopar engineers went back to the wind tunnel and emerged with the Charger Daytona. Instead of a flush nose, it wore a pointed 18-inch extension. It retained the 500's flush backlight, but added a tail stabilizer on tall vertical extensions. Here a street car and the prototype racer share the test track. Note the differences in the shapes of the nose cones and rear wings; the white street car wears the production pieces.

▲ 1969 DODGE
CHARGER DAYTONA

The Charger Daytona made its track debut at Talladega in September 1969. Only two of the winged warriors took part in the race, but Richard Brickhouse won in one of them. To make the car eligible for competition, Dodge had to again build street versions, and about 505 were offered for sale to the public. The street cars were equipped much like a Charger R/T. The 440 Magnum was standard, with the 426 Hemi optional. The winged Daytona weighed about 300 pounds more than a standard Charger, so acceleration and handling were negatively affected. But the Daytona's real impact was as the muscle car taken to its magnificent extreme.

▶ *1969 PLYMOUTH*
'CUDA

A new 'Cuda option package transformed Plymouth's sporty compact into a true muscle machine. 'Cudas were easy to spot with their blacked-out grilles, black striping, engine-size callouts, and a pair of small nonfunctional hood scoops. At the beginning of the model year, the 340 and 383 engines were the only choices. In April, the 375-horse 440 was added to the mix. The big engine left no room in the engine bay for power steering or power brakes, making the nose-heavy car less than ideal to drive on the street.

◀ *1969 PLYMOUTH*
ROAD RUNNER

Plymouth had some of the muscle era's most evocative advertising art, conveying in carica-ture the power and personality of its muscle cars. By '69, the artwork's tone had evolved from love-in bright to the darker, acid-trip style so wonderfully represented here.

▶ *1969 PLYMOUTH*
ROAD RUNNER

With the Road Runner accounting for 35 per-cent of its midsize-car sales, Plymouth didn't tamper much with the winning formula as set out in the '68 original. A convertible joined the hardtop and pillared coupe, the grille and taillamps were revised, and the bird insignia were now in full color. A center console, front buckets, and power windows were added to the options list. Sales exploded to 84,420, nearly doubling the '68 figure.

▼ *1969 PLYMOUTH*
ROAD RUNNER 440+6

At the start of '69 Road Runner production, the 335-hp 383 remained standard, with the only upgrade being the 426 Hemi. Midyear, buyers got a third choice, the same triple-carb 440 V-8 that debuted in the '69 Dodge Super Bee. In a Road Runner, it was called "440+6" and it came with a big-scoop, lift-off fiberglass hood in flat black, Hurst shifter, and a 4.10:1 Sure-Grip rear end. The 390-horsepower 440+6 provided Hemi-style acceleration for about half the price.

▼ *1970 DODGE*
CHALLENGER R/T

It took Chrysler six years to develop a true ponycar, and by time the 1970 Dodge Challenger was introduced, it was difficult to do anything really new with the formula. Offering an astonishing range of engine choices, from a docile slant six to the earthshaking Hemi, was Dodge's way of getting attention. Challenger used the same unibody platform as Plymouth's redesigned Barracuda, but with a two-inch-longer wheelbase. It was sold in hardtop and convertible form, with performance versions wearing the familiar R/T label.

▲ *1969 PLYMOUTH*
GTX HEMI

Entering its third season, GTX styling was tidied up in detail, while the basic package—heavy-duty suspension/shocks/brakes, chrome engine trim, and an unsilenced air cleaner—was retained. The Super Commando 440 remained standard, with the Hemi optional; the Road Runner's 440+6 engine was not a GTX offering. New options included the Air Grabber hood. It was not a hood scoop, but rather an air intake that allowed cool outside air to reach the engine.

▲ *1970 DODGE*
CHALLENGER R/T 440 SIX PACK

Standard R/T power came from the 335-horse 383. Two 440s were offered: the four-barrel Magnum with 375 ponies and the tri-carb Six Pack with 390. The 425-horsepower 426 Hemi cost $1228 with required heavy-duty equipment. The 440s and the Hemi came standard with Torque-Flite automatic. Ordering the four-speed brought a pistol-grip Hurst shifter and a Dana 60 rear axle. The R/T's standard hood had two scoops that were open but didn't feed directly to the air cleaner. A $97 option was the shaker scoop, which mounted to the air cleaner and protruded through an opening in the hood. *Road Test* said of its Six Pack Challenger, "The car squirts forward like an unleashed dragster…and suddenly you're way above the speed limit…."

1970 DODGE
CHALLENGER R/T HEMI

Hemis were the quickest Challengers, but not by enough to justify their significant price premium over the next-most-potent iteration, the 440 Six Pack. All R/Ts had a beefed suspension, and 440 and Hemi cars got 15-inch 60-series tires, though such essentials as power steering and front disc brakes were optional. Dodge sold 83,032 Challengers for 1970. Of 19,938 R/Ts, 356 were Hemis, and 2035 were Six Packs. While this R/T is free of stripes, "bumblebee" or longitudinal stripes were a no-cost R/T option.

1970 DODGE
CHALLENGER T/A

Dodge entered the Challenger in the Sports Car Club of America's Trans American Sedan Championship, popularly known as Trans-Am. Rules required automakers to sell production versions of their track cars, and Dodge responded with the Challenger T/A. The street cars ran a 340 topped with a trio of two-barrel Holleys atop an Edelbrock intake. It carried the same 290-horsepower rating as standard four-barrel 340s, though true output was near 350. A matte-black scooped fiberglass hood, side-exit dual exhausts, special striping, and front and rear spoilers were included.

▼ *1970 DODGE*
DART SWINGER 340

Dodge's Dart compacts wore fresh front and rear styling for 1970. On the performance front, the previous top-dog GTS was discontinued, leaving the Swinger 340 to take its place. The lone engine choice was Mopar's well-regarded 340 small block, here rated at 275 horsepower. The Swinger 340 was only offered in hardtop form and came standard with a pair of nonfunctional hood scoops. Other standard items included an upgraded suspension, E70×14 tires, chrome exhaust tips, and a bumblebee stripe. Extras included all-vinyl bucket seats, center console, and styled steel "Rallye" wheels. The Swinger 340 drew 13,785 orders.

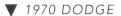

▼ *1970 DODGE*
CORONET R/T

The '70 Coronets remained on a 117-inch wheelbase, but the styling changes added three inches to the overall length. Coronet R/Ts looked much like the cheaper Super Bee from the front, but side scoops aft of the rear doors and a flat-black rear panel with triple-section taillamps provided some visual distinction. The Super Bee's 440 Six Pack engine was now optional on the R/T. The popularity of the muscular Coronets was waning. Super Bee production fell by nearly half, to 14,254. R/Ts registered a paltry 2408 sales.

▲ *1970 DODGE*
CORONET SUPER BEE

An extensive facelift was approved for the 1970 Coronets, most obviously highlighted by a controversial double-delta loop bumper up front. Each loop housed a pair of headlamps and vertical grille bars. Performance models had a new dual-inlet power bulge on the hood. Optional Ramcharger air induction with twin scoops remained an extra-cost choice. At the rear, horizontally split taillamps recalled the look of the new front bumper/grille units. Super Bees still came with a standard 383. The 440 Six Pack and Hemi were the only engine options.

▲ *1970 DODGE*
CHARGER R/T

For 1970, Chargers had a new loop front bumper that was echoed by a full-width taillamp housing. R/T versions gained simulated reverse-facing scoops at the leading edge of the doors. Inside, new highback front seats were Charger's first true buckets, and a hip pistol-grip handle topped the available four-speed Hurst shifter. Again, R/Ts had the 375-horsepower 440 standard and the Hemi optional. These were joined by the 440 Six Pack with 390 ponies. R/T production fell by nearly half, to 10,337. With 116 orders, the 440 Six Pack outsold the Hemi by more than two to one.

1970 PLYMOUTH
HEMI 'CUDA

The Barracuda, Plymouth's sports compact since 1964, finally stepped away from its Valiant roots for 1970. Its broad-shouldered long hood/short deck "E-body" platform was shared with the new Dodge Challenger. Hardtop coupes and convertibles were available in base, plush Gran Coupe, and racy 'Cuda series. The 'Cuda, which took its name from enthusiasts' slang for Barracuda, started with a 335-horse 383 hooked to a three-speed manual transmission. Options included 340 and 440 V-8s and a choice of four-speed or Torque-Flite automatic transmissions. The Barracuda with the sharpest teeth was the Hemi 'Cuda. It came stuffed with 426 inches of pure Mopar muscle under a "shaker" hood scoop.

1970 PLYMOUTH
AAR 'CUDA

Like Dodge, Plymouth needed an homologation special to be able to run in the Trans-Am series. The AAR 'Cuda did the trick. Named for and inspired by Dan Gurney's All-American Racers team that ran the 'Cudas in Trans-Am, the AAR came with a beefed-up 340 with triple two-barrel carburetion and side-exit exhausts, a setup that generated 290 horsepower. Other specific touches included a fiberglass hood with functional scoop, a ducktail spoiler on the decklid, and a jacked-up rear-end to accommodate large rear tires. Street handling was emphasized, but *Car and Driver*'s AAR with the standard four-speed and 3.55:1 rear gears still ran a quick 14.3 in the quarter at 99.5 mph. The AAR started at $3966, some $800 above a base 'Cuda coupe. Only 2724 were built.

1970 PLYMOUTH
HEMI 'CUDA

Chrysler engineers fitted the Hemi with hydraulic lifters for 1970. The result was that it was easier to maintain and, according to some testers, had improved low-rpm power. Compared to the $871 Hemi, the 440+6 was a bargain at $250. Both came with a Hurst pistol-grip four-speed or TorqueFlite and a extra-heavy-duty Dana axle. The 440+6 could stay with a Hemi to about 70 mph or so. That might be enough from a stoplight, but not in really serious action, where the race-bred 426 was in its element. Nobody handed this engine its reputation. It earned it.

1970 PLYMOUTH
'CUDA 383

Against the 1967-69 Barracudas, the redesigned '70 was two inches lower, three inches wider, a tad shorter, much heavier, and somehow more conventional looking. The convertible was available in three forms: base, performance-oriented 'Cuda, and luxury Gran Coupe. The later was a bit awkward since it resulted in a Gran Coupe convertible. Only 635 'Cuda ragtops were built, and of those a mere 14 had the Hemi. This 383-powered convertible has the optional rear spoiler and body-color front bumper.

▶ *1970 PLYMOUTH*
'CUDA

Ronnie Sox (left) and Buddy Martin with the Super Stock Hemi 'Cuda that took them to their most successful season. The team won 17 major drag events in '70. Sox was the wheelman in 13 of them; Herb McCandless handled the rest. Their Hemi had 13.5:1 compression, Holley dual quads, an experimental camshaft, and transistorized ignition. Valves were the stock size: 2.25-inch intake, 1.94-inch exhaust. The car weighed 2980 pounds ready to rock.

▶ *1970 PLYMOUTH*
DUSTER 340

Just as it had with the '68 Road Runner, Plymouth scored a budget-muscle bull's-eye in 1970 with the Duster 340. The formula was familiar. Take a cheap-to-produce model, in this case a Valiant wearing an attractive new fastback body, and treat it to a hot engine, here the respected 340 four-barrel. The determined little Duster was lighter, roomier, and faster than a 340 'Cuda. With a base price of just $2547, it was the lowest priced car in Plymouth's Rapid Transit System (the brand's answer to Dodge's Scat Pack). This car wears an extra-cost "High-Impact" color called Moulin Rouge.

◀ *1970 PLYMOUTH*
ROAD RUNNER

Plymouth's intermediates finished their 1968-70 styling cycle with freshened sheetmetal, including handsome loop-motif front and rear ends and dummy rear-fender scoops. Inside, there was a revised dashboard and new buckets. Muscle-age marketing was a treat, and some of the most entertaining was from Dodge and Plymouth. Rife with op-art graphics, flower-power imagery, and brilliant colors, they were an unabashed reflection of the times. The '70 Road Runner, for example, was introduced with a photo showing a giant, three-dimensional sculpture of its goofy cartoon namesake emerging from its cool pop-up hood scoop.

▼ *1970 PLYMOUTH*
SUPERBIRD

Though it was a virtual twin to the Charger Daytona in concept, the Superbird's aerodynamic add-ons were unique parts developed expressly for the 1970 Road Runner body. It was an exercise in savvy corporate parts swapping and cost-cutting ingenuity. The Superbird's special front nose cone was fitted to the front fenders and a lengthened hood from the 1970 Dodge Coronet. All production Superbirds wore vinyl tops to hide the welding seams left by the fitment of a flush-mount rear window. As if the huge rear wing and wind-tunnel-shaped snout weren't enough, Plymouth added big cartoon Road Runner graphics, flat black panels on the nose, and billboard-size "Plymouth" stickers for more visual punch.

▲ *1970 PLYMOUTH*
SUPERBIRD

In 1969, Plymouth lacked a suitable aerodynamic machine for battle on the nation's super speedways. In response, Plymouth stalwart Richard Petty did the unthinkable and jumped ship to Ford. To lure him back into the fold for 1970, Plymouth created its own "winged warrior" clearly inspired by the 1969 Dodge Charger Daytona. Based on the Road Runner, the slippery creation was called the Superbird. Superbirds accounted for eight big-track victories in 1970; Petty was at the wheel for five of them.

▼ *1970 PLYMOUTH*
SUPERBIRD

Dodge was required to build a minimum of 500 street-legal Charger Daytonas in order for NASCAR to allow the car to race. A rule change for 1970 meant Plymouth had to make half as many Superbirds as the marque had dealers. That meant about 1900 needed to be built. The final total isn't known, but 1920 is a commonly accepted figure. This many Superbirds proved to be a tough sell, and dealers struggled to move them. The photo shows Superbirds flocked together following final assembly at a Detroit-area Chrysler facility.

▲ *1970 PLYMOUTH*
GTX

In 1970, buyers began turning away from muscle cars in the face of rising insurance premiums and gas prices, but the GTX was still around for those who wanted a hot Plymouth with creature comforts. For '70, it was only offered as a hardtop. The 440 with 375 horsepower was still standard. The 440+6 was a new GTX option, and the mighty 426 Hemi was still available too. The year's styling was especially handsome in GTX trim. The blackout grille was echoed on the restyled rear end, and the bodyside striping ran into the simulated rear-fender scoops.

1971 DODGE
CHALLENGER R/T

The Challenger returned for 1971 with only minor appearance and mechanical changes. The line was trimmed to a base hardtop and convertible, along with the R/T hardtop. All were marked by a reworked grille and taillamps. The R/T also received body-color bumpers, simulated brake cooling scoops on the rear quarters, and revised tape striping with large ID lettering on the bodysides near the C-pillars and on the nose. Power ratings were now quoted in SAE net figures instead of the old gross horsepower, though actual outputs weren't affected. Thus, the 383 Magnum came down from its previous 335-horsepower gross rating to 250 net. Chrysler did not drop compression ratios in '71 like General Motors did, and Challengers with the big 440 and Hemi engines were still stunningly fast. Still, Challenger sales fell dramatically for 1971; the model year total of 29,883 was down by more than 60 percent. Other ponycars suffered too; the market was shrinking quickly as federal safety and emissions standards proliferated and Madison Avenue's beloved baby boomers—the prime ponycar prospects—turned from "road appearance" value to more practical concerns.

◀ 1971 DODGE
CHALLENGER INDY 500 PACE CAR

With the R/T convertible discontinued, all '71 Challenger ragtops were base models. Four Dodge dealers attempted to spur interest in the Challenger by agreeing to supply cars for the 1971 Indianapolis 500 pace car program. It is believed 50 Hemi Orange convertibles were prepared for use during pre-race festivities. Two of the Challengers were equipped with heavy-duty tires and other equipment, one as the actual pace car, the other as a backup. During the parade lap, the pace car—loaded with dignitaries—went into a skid as it was leaving the track and crashed into a press box, injuring several reporters.

▶ *1971 DODGE*
DEMON 340

Dodge introduced the sporty Demon compact for 1971. Demon was basically a Plymouth Duster body with Dodge Dart sheetmetal in front and redesigned taillamps in the back. As Plymouth did with the Duster 340, Dodge offered a mini-muscle Demon 340. As in other Mopars, it packed a 275-horse 340 four barrel. Plenty of muscle-car visual cues were available too, including a twin-scooped hood and Rallye wheels. At $2721 to start, it was a devilish value.

▶ *1971 DODGE*
CHARGER R/T

The 1971 Charger was a radical departure from its predecessor, losing two inches of wheelbase and gaining Coke-bottle contours. The R/T remained the performance leader, and it stayed true to its roots with a daunting underhood lineup. The 370-horsepower 440 Magnum was standard, with the 385-horse 440 Six Pack available at extra cost. Topping the lineup was the Hemi, still good for 425 race-bred ponies. Non-Hemi R/Ts like this 440 came standard with nonfunctional hood louvers. Hideaway headlamps were optional.

◀ *1971 DODGE*
CHARGER R/T

A blackout hood graphic, tape stripes, Rallye wheels, and special door skins with simulated air extractors rounded out the Charger R/T appearance features. High-impact colors and spoilers on the rear deck and chin were optional. Base price on the Charger R/T was $3777. Production ran only 3118 units. Just 85 had the mighty Hemi.

▶ *1971 DODGE*
CHARGER SUPER BEE

All of Dodge's intermediate two-door were Chargers for 1971, and the Coronet name was assigned solely to four-doors and wagon. One side effect of this model shuffling was the transfer of Coronet's budget-muscle Super Bee version to the redesigned Charger. Super Bees came standard with the 300-horsepower 383, detuned so the four-barrel engine could run on regular-grade gas. This example wears the optional "Ramcharger" hood with a vacuum-operated pop-up scoop. At $3271 to start, the Super Bee undercut an R/T by $506. Dealers were able to move 5054 of them out of the hive.

◀ *1971 PLYMOUTH*
'CUDA 340

Chrysler's 1970 ponycars were muscle styling masterpieces, with crisp long-hood/short-deck proportions and a wide sinister stance. For '71, Barracudas got revised taillights and a busy grille with quad headlights and six "venturi" air inlets. The performance-oriented 'Cuda variants amped up the ostentation with hood pins, chrome front-fender "gills," twin-scooped hood, and a host of "look at me" options.

▶ *1971 PLYMOUTH*
'CUDA 383

Popular 'Cuda add-ons included the shaker hood scoop, rear spoiler, and wild "billboard" bodyside stripes that called out engine size. For the time being, there was still plenty of go to match all of this show. 'Cudas again featured 340, 383, 440, and 426 Hemi power, though the 440 was now available only in six-barrel form. Still, it was clear by the end of 1971 that the 'Cuda was a fish out of water. Barracuda sales plummeted by 66 percent for the model year as the ponycar market quickly faded.

▶ *1971 PLYMOUTH*
'CUDA

While some of 'Cuda's rivals dialed back on performance to appease emissions and insurance concerns, Plymouth still offered a broad muscle range. Also back was the shaker scoop, as seen on this 440 six-barrel convertible. Standard on Hemis, optional on other 'Cuda mills, this functional piece mounted directly to the air cleaner assembly and shook through a hole in the hood as the engine rocked.

◀ *1971 PLYMOUTH*
HEMI 'CUDA

Total Barracuda production for 1971 was 18,690. Convertibles accounted for only 1388 sales, and a mere 374 of the ragtops were 'Cudas. Given generally low take rates for Hemis, it might be surprising that 11 'Cuda convertibles were optioned with the 425-horsepower 426 engine. For a long time, historians believed the total was nine, but it was discovered that two additional Hemi 'Cuda convertibles had been exported to France. This Winchester Gray metallic example is one of the French cars. It has a four-speed; the other was an automatic.

▶ *1971 PLYMOUTH*
DUSTER

Capitalizing on the popularity of the original Duster 340 was a decidedly less muscular Duster Twister, seen here in Sassy Grass Green. Twister got the 340's grille, mirrors, and wheels (without trim rings). The blackout, strobe-stripe hood was standard, but the nonfunctional scoops were extra. Twisters were offered with a pair of six-cylinder engines or a 230-horsepower 318-cubic-inch two-barrel V-8. Plymouth noted that these engines made the Twister easier to insure and cheaper to fuel than the 340.

▶ *1971 PLYMOUTH*
ROAD RUNNER

Plymouth's Rapid Transit System continued service in 1971 with a radically restyled Road Runner. Wheelbase dropped an inch, to 115, the rear track was widened by three inches for better handling, and the interior was reconfigured to allow for a more comfortable driving position. The only body style was a hardtop coupe. Bold color choices extended to Road Runner's interior for 1971, with the introduction of optional black-and-orange seat trim.

◀ *1971 PLYMOUTH*
ROAD RUNNER HEMI

Road Runner started '71 with 383, 440+6, and 426 Hemi engine choices. During the year, a 275-horsepower 340 was also made available as the Road Runner's first small-block engine. Options included a body-color elastomeric front bumper and Air Grabber hood with pop-up scoop. Despite the new skin, Road Runner sales plummeted from 41,484 to 14,218 in '71. Only 55 of them packed the 426 Hemi.

▶ *1971 PLYMOUTH*
GTX

This was the final year for the GTX, but it died with its big-cube boots on. The 440 was still standard, and the Hemi optional. The GTX remained at the top of Plymouth's price-and-performance hill at $3733 to start. Standard features included TorqueFlite, bucket seats, low-restriction dual exhausts with chrome tips, dual horns, raised-white-letter tires, and heavy-duty suspension and brakes. The wild stripes that ran from the simulated hood scoops over each front fender were extra.

▼ 1971 PLYMOUTH
GTX

Plymouth said all its intermediates had new "Fuselage Styling" for 1971, but the two-doors wore it best. From the rear the semi-fastback profile is visible, and note the segmented tail-lamps set into the massive rear bumper. This GTX wears the optional rear-window louvers and trunk-mounted rear spoiler. Production fell to 2942. Only 30 buyers ponied up for the Hemi.

▼ 1972 DODGE
CHALLENGER

Challenger appearance was altered with a new "sad mouth" grille up front, and four smaller, rectangular taillamps out back. Rallyes had a tame 318 as the standard engine. The only upgrade was a new low-compression 340 rated at 240 horsepower. The bigger motor could be ordered with a Performance Axle option including 3.55:1 final drive, Sure-Grip differential, and increased cooling capacity. Sales were down a bit further to 26,663.

▲ 1972 DODGE
CHALLENGER

Challenger entered its third model year for 1972, and the offerings mirrored the new market realities. Convertibles were gone, along with the Scat Pack, the R/T, and all of the big-block engines including the Hemi. There were now only two models. The base hardtop listed at $2790, with the Rallye about $300 upstream. The latter was really a "cosmetic muscle car," sporting simulated air extractors on the front fenders, from which tape stripes flowed rearward. It also had F70×14 tires and a "performance" hood.

▲ 1972 DODGE
CHARGER RALLYE

For 1972, Charger lost the Super Bee, the R/T, the Ramcharger hood, and the Hemi. The buyers still looking for performance could choose the new Rallye option. It included a heavy-duty suspension, power bulge hood, louvered taillamps, and other styling fillips. These included large oblong dummy exhaust vents stacked on the doors like little enemy flags on a fighter plane's fuselage. The Rallye's standard engine was a 318 with 150 horsepower. How the mighty had fallen! Upgrades included a 240-horse 340 and a 440 that was good for 280 ponies.

▲ *1972 PLYMOUTH*

'CUDA

At Plymouth, performance offerings dwindled very much like they did at Dodge. The Barracuda convertible and all the big-block engines were discontinued. 'Cudas remained the performance model, but like Challenger a 318 two-barrel was standard, and the 240-horse 340 was the only upgrade. Styling was tweaked. Up front, the car reverted to a two-headlamp face, flanking a grille that recalled the look used in 1970. In the rear, four round taillamps took station. 'Cudas still had the two-scoop hood, but the shaker was gone for good. Total Barracuda production held almost steady at 18,450 units. Of that number, 7828 were the defanged 'Cudas.

▼ *1973 DODGE*

CHALLENGER RALLYE

Challenger saw few changes for '73. The most obvious was the addition of large solid-rubber pads to the front bumper to meet the new government-ordered 5-mph impact standard. The Rallye, a separate model in '72, was downgraded to a $182 option package for the lone base-model Challenger. The interior boasted new thin-shell bucket seats. The 318 was now standard on all Challengers (the slant six was previously included on base cars). The lone upgrade was the 340, which could propel a Challenger with TorqueFlite through the quarter mile in 16.3 seconds at 85 mph. Not bad for 1973.

▼ *1972 PLYMOUTH*

ROAD RUNNER

This was the last year the Road Runner had anything like the original's sizzle. The base engine was now a 400-cube big-block, essentially a bored-out 383. It was good for 255 horsepower. Like the available 340, the 400 breathed through Carter's novel plastic-bodied Thermo-Quad carb. Though Plymouth's plush GTX was gone, the '72 Road Runner could be had with a "GTX option"—a four-barrel 440 making 280 horsepower.

▼ *1973 DODGE*

DART SPORT 340

The Demon was gone for 1973, replaced by a lightly restyled, unimaginatively renamed Dart Sport. This factory publicity photo shows a Dart Sport 340 smoking the rear tires, apparently an attempt to demonstrate that the Dodge Boys still had a bit of muscle up their sleeves. Only 11,315 Dart Sport 340s were sold, priced from an affordable $2793.

▼ 1973 DODGE
CHARGER

Charger wasn't really a muscle car anymore, but as a mainstream product it remained a success. Sales didn't drop out of sight like they had for so many rivals; actually, the '73 Charger set a production record of nearly 120,000 units. The minor changes for '73 included a new grille (no more hidden headlights), 22-segment taillights, and revised rear-quarter windows. With luxury coupes becoming the new sales champs, the Charger SE—complete with stand-up hood ornament, six opera windows, and a landau vinyl roof—accounted for more than half the sales.

▼ 1973 PLYMOUTH
DUSTER 340

The Duster wore a handsome facelift for 1973. Beyond that, the big news was a proliferation of special nameplates, none particularly muscular. A luxury package made the Duster into a Gold Duster. Add an optional sunroof and a fold-down rear seat and you had a Space Duster. If you were one of the few who wanted more than a mild-mannered 318 in your Plymouth compact, you really only had one choice: the Duster 340. It still had 240 horsepower.

▲ 1973 PLYMOUTH
BARRACUDA

At Plymouth, Barracudas changed little for 1973. Base cars no longer carried a standard 225-cubic-inch slant six; a 318 V-8 was now found under the flat hood. 'Cudas still came with the 340 and dual-scooped hood. Base prices were $2935 for Barracuda and $3120 for 'Cuda. Total production perked up to 22,213. The base car was slightly more popular with 11,587 sold.

▲ 1973 PLYMOUTH
DUSTER 340

Duster production was 249,243 for 1973, with the Duster 340 selling an additional 15,731 units. With muscle fading fast, some of the big performance dealers were doing their best to evolve with the times. In Chicago, Mr. Norm's Grand-Spaulding Dodge developed a GSS Supercharger kit for the 1972 Demon. The Paxton-blown GSS Demons were drag-strip terrors that some said were capable of running high 12s in the quarter on slicks. Though Mr. Norm's sold Dodges, this 1973 Duster has been fitted with the blower setup.

▲ 1973 PLYMOUTH
ROAD RUNNER

For 1973, Plymouth's Road Runner was still going, in name if not in spirit, at a time when other hot cars were pooping out like . . . well, old Wile E. Coyote. Reduced competition, plus a still-reasonable $3095 starting price may help explain why Road Runner sales recovered to 19,056. Under the bulged hood, Road Runner suffered the indignity of receiving a 170-horsepower two-barrel 318 as its new standard engine.

▲ 1974 DODGE
CHALLENGER RALLYE

Reluctant to spend any more money on it than absolutely necessary, Dodge did little to the Challenger for 1974. Rear bumpers were strengthened to withstand 5-mph shunts as the government said they must, and the Rallye package was revised with a black-painted grille and "strobe" stripes trailing from the fake fender vents. Substituting for the 340 as the "performance" option was a new 360-cubic-inch V-8 rated at 245 horsepower.

▼ 1973 PLYMOUTH
ROAD RUNNER

Road Runner's 1973 restyle was handsome, in a chunky sort of way. Big rubber bumper guards helped the car meet the new government crash standards. Though Road Runner performance wasn't close to even 1971 levels, some Mopar muscle was still available on the options list. The 340 still delivered 240 horsepower, a 400 brought 255 ponies, and the big 440 soldiered on at 280. The Air Grabber hood option was no longer available. The 340 and 400 engines could be backed by a four-speed transmission, complete with a Hurst pistol-grip shifter.

▼ 1974 DODGE
CHALLENGER RALLYE

The '74 was on the market for only a few months before Dodge suddenly pulled the plug on the Challenger, and only 16,437 units made it to the end of the assembly line. The Challenger wasn't so much a weak entry in the ponycar field as it was a late one. It appeared just as demand for such cars was starting to evaporate, which clearly diluted whatever impact it might have had. Of course, Dodge couldn't have predicted this market switch when it was planning the Challenger in 1967.

▲ 1974 PLYMOUTH
'CUDA

The Barracuda also entered its final year in 1974. The only major change was the 360 V-8 replacing the 340. That was hardly cause for celebration, however, since the substitution was clearly an economy move. The 360 had not been designed as a high-performance powerplant, and Mopar enthusiasts knew that. Still, it would move. Rated at 245 horsepower, the 360 came standard on 'Cuda and was a $259 option on the base fish. But time ran out on the Barracuda in 1974. Just 11,734 examples were made, an ignominious end for a fine little automobile.

▼ 1974 PLYMOUTH
ROAD RUNNER

Road Runner carried on with minor changes for 1974. The 318 was still standard. Like other Mopars, the old optional 340 was replaced with the 360. The 440 four-barrel was still available, but now with 275 horsepower. Visual indicators of performance like the bird decals, hood bulge, and tape stripes continued, but former standard features like a performance rear axle and heavy-duty suspension were now options. Road Runner sales totaled 11,555.

▼ 1974 PLYMOUTH
DUSTER

Duster remained the most popular Plymouth for 1974. The sunroof and fold-down rear seat mark this one as a Space Duster. The package was likely Plymouth's response to compact hatchbacks like the AMC Hornet and Chevy Nova. The performance model became Duster 360, thanks to its new engine.

▲ 1975 PLYMOUTH
ROAD RUNNER

For 1975, Plymouth unveiled a totally redesigned—and renamed—range of midsizers. The Satellite moniker was dropped, replaced by the Fury name appropriated from Plymouth's full-size cars (which were renamed Gran Fury). Road Runner was now an option for the base Fury coupe. The blocky styling was a snooze, as was the standard 318 backed by a three-speed stick. The four-speed and the 440 were history, leaving a 235-horse 400 as the top engine option.

▲ *1977 DODGE*
ASPEN R/T SUPER PAK

Chrysler redesigned its compacts for 1976. Dodge's version was called Aspen. This was the era of "tape-stripe muscle," where looking cool on the street was more important than moving down the strip. Dodge dusted off the R/T nameplate for the "performance" Aspen. Slant six was standard in Aspen, but R/Ts were V-8 only with 318- and 360-cube versions available, the latter with 175 horsepower. This Aspen R/T also has the Super Pak option, which added front and rear spoilers, wheel flares, and louvered rear-quarter windows. Hot stuff for 1977.

▲ *1978 DODGE*
ASPEN SUPER COUPE

In 1978, Dodge brought out the Super Coupe, described as "a super Aspen" by the catalog copywriters. It came only in dark brown, with contrasting satin black hood, bumpers, lower body, plus huge wheel flares and a rear spoiler. Orange and blue stripes added to the racetrack look, which was backed up with 15×8-inch GT wheels, GR60 white-letter radials, rear anti-sway bar, and a 360 four-barrel.

▼ *1977 PLYMOUTH*
VOLARÉ ROAD RUNNER SUPER PAK

Plymouth's new compact was the 1976 Volaré. After one year as a Fury option, Road Runner migrated to the Volaré in '76. For 1977, the Road Runner was included in a group of two-door Volarés the marketing types called the "Fun Runners." At the top of this heap was Road Runner. Its standard 318 was good for 150 horses, and could be backed up by three- or four-speed manuals, or the TorqueFlite automatic. The 360 was still around at 175 ponies, but it only came with the automatic. Road Runners with the Super Pak option added front and rear spoilers, wheel flares, and quarter-window louvers.

▼ *1978 DODGE*
ASPEN R/T SPORT PACK

Like its linemates, the 1978 Aspen R/T wore a mild facelift that included a new grille and larger taillights. Positioned below the Super Coupe but above the R/T in the Aspen lineup was the renamed R/T Sport Pack. All show, it added a front air dam, wheel flares, quarter window louvers, and a rear deck spoiler. It only came in black or white, each with tricolor stripes.

▼ 1978 PLYMOUTH
VOLARÉ ROAD RUNNER & SUPER COUPE

Volaré was lightly facelifted for 1978 too, with the most obvious tweaks being a new grille and taillamps. Road Runners wore revised striping in bright colors, and the Sport Pack added spoilers and flares, along with revised quarter-window louvers. Not surprisingly, Plymouth got a version of the Super Coupe too. The stripes were brighter and the main body color was different, but otherwise Plymouth's Super Coupe execution was darn near the same as Dodge's. Less than 500 were made.

▲ 1978 PLYMOUTH
VOLARÉ STREET KIT CAR

Volaré coupe buyers were also offered a "Street Kit Car" option package for $1085. The package was inspired by the "Kit Car," a "build-it-yourself" short-track race-car kit prepared in Richard Petty's race shop and sold through Chrysler. The street version added bolt-on fender flares, a big rear spoiler, metal window straps, and large "43" (Richard Petty's race number) graphics on the roof and doors. All were finished in two-tone blue paint. Perhaps predictably, Dodge offered a Street Kit Car Aspen that looked nearly the same except for two-tone red paint. Reportedly, Plymouth sold 247 Street Kit Cars and Dodge dealers moved about 145.

▼ 1979 DODGE
ASPEN R/T

Aspen changed little for 1979, but the optional $651 R/T package added new strobe-pattern striping on the hood, taillight panel, and lower body. R/Ts also added a three-piece rear spoiler, quarter-window louvers, dual sport mirrors, and cast aluminum wheels. R/Ts required an optional V-8, with the top choice still the 360.

▲ 1979 DODGE
MAGNUM GT

The market for midsize two-doors moved from high-performance to "personal luxury" during the Seventies. The Dodge Charger adapted better than most by migrating to a posher platform shared with Chrysler Cordoba for 1975. Still, the Chrysler outsold the '75 Charger by nearly five-to-one. By 1978, the Cordoba-based Dodge Charger was joined by the new Magnum. Magnum's claim to fame was a simple louvered grille and clear headlight covers that retracted when the lamps were in use. Most Magnums were XE models that traded primarily on luxury. Buyers looking for a bit more performance could choose the Magnum GT with 15×7 wheels, raised-white-letter radials, retuned suspension, and engine-turned dashboard trim. Unlike lesser Magnums, the GT could be ordered with a 360 four-barrel with 195 horsepower. Magnum disappeared for 1980, replaced by the Mirada. Rear-drive Mopar performance thus entered a long, deep hibernation.

▲ *2005 CHRYSLER*
300C SRT-8

For 2003, Chrysler Corporation released a brand new 5.7-liter "Hemi" V-8. It was first used in the Dodge Ram pickup. Mopar-muscle fans had to wait a bit for a reprised Hemi-powered passenger car. That happened for 2005, when the Chrysler 300C launched with a 340-horse-power version of the 5.7 Hemi. Higher performance arrived with the midyear 300C SRT-8. SRT stands for "Street and Racing Technology," a label given to Chrysler's highest-performance vehicles. The 300C SRT-8 packed a 425-horsepower, 6.1-liter version of the Hemi. In a nod to the old 426, the 6.1's engine block was painted orange.

▼ *2006 DODGE*
CHARGER R/T

Charger, one of Dodge's greatest nameplates of the muscle years, was reduced to duty on front-drive subcompacts during the 1980s. Dormant for years, the moniker reappeared for Dodge's 2006 full-size four-door sedan that shared much of the Chrysler 300's chassis. Aware that muscle car purists would balk at the body style, Dodge called it a "coupe-styled sedan." Base Chargers had a 3.5-liter V-6, but R/T versions packed the 340-hp 5.7 Hemi. The available Road/Track Performance Group added suspension upgrades and bumped hp to 350.

▼ *2006 DODGE*
CHALLENGER CONCEPT

Debuting at the 2006 Detroit Auto Show was the Dodge Challenger Concept, a new-millennium re-imagining of the legendary 1970 original. It was built on a shortened Charger/300C chassis. Like the Camaro Concept introduced at the same show, enthusiasts said "Build it!" and Dodge announced in July that it would. The production version that arrived for 2008 stayed remarkably true to the show car, though details such as the rear-fender name badge and "gun sight" grille didn't make the cut.

▲ *2006 DODGE*
CHARGER DAYTONA

Dodge tapped further into muscle car lore with the 2006 Charger Daytona. It was offered in two "High Impact"-inspired colors; Top Banana and Go ManGo. Distinguishing the Daytona from other Chargers were chin and deck spoilers, flat black accents on the hood and trunk panels, rear fender stripes with "Daytona" lettering, and old-school R/T badges. Daytonas had special Hemi Orange engine covers, along with tweaked intake and exhaust systems that gave them 350 horsepower. Like the 340-horse version, Daytona's Hemi featured Dodge's Multi-Displacement System, which shut down four cylinders while cruising and idling to improve fuel economy.

▼ *2006 DODGE*
MAGNUM SRT-8

Dodge introduced the Chrysler 300-based Magnum station wagon for 2005. Already quite capable with the 5.7 Hemi, Magnum added a SRT-8 version for 2006. Dodge's stated goal was to create "a vehicle that can cover the quarter mile in the high 13-second range and haul home a brand-new 27-inch TV." Along with a 425-horsepower 6.1-liter Hemi, it had a specific front fascia, large Brembo brakes with red calipers, a sport-tuned suspension, and 20-inch wheels.

▲ *2007 DODGE*
CHARGER SRT8 SUPER BEE

Given the muscle-car heritage of the Charger name, it came as no surprise when Dodge gave the Charger its own SRT version for 2006. Charger SRT8 got several visual and performance mods, including a new front fascia, a functional hood scoop, 20-inch wheels, and, of course, 425 horses in the 6.1-liter Hemi. For 2007, the SRT8 could be ordered with a Super Bee package that included Detonator Yellow paint and hard-to-miss graphics.

2008 DODGE
CHALLENGER SRT8

Chrysler took the unusual step of debuting the hotly anticipated production 2008 Dodge Challenger in top-line SRT8 trim only. Sticker price was $37,995, but buyers also had to cough up for a $2100 gas-guzzler tax. Just three colors were available: Hemi Orange, Bright Silver Metallic, and Brilliant Black Crystal Pearl Coat. Under its retro-styled skin, the Challenger SRT8 was a shortened Chrysler 300C with a tighter suspension, a 6.1-liter Hemi, 425 horsepower, 420 pound-feet of torque, and 0-60 times clocked at a hair over five seconds. Not just ferociously powerful, Challenger was also a pleasant and quiet highway cruiser. One big drawback for muscle enthusiasts was the mandatory five-speed automatic; no manual transmission was available . . . yet.

▶ *2008 DODGE*
MAGNUM SRT8

Dodge's baddest hot-rod wagon entered 2008 with a mildly reworked interior and a restyled front end with a new fascia and smaller headlamps. There was a new hood scoop too, though the 6.1-liter Hemi stood pat at 425 horsepower. While the wagon body added surprising utility, Magnum sales really never took off. Gas prices ran up to record levels during 2008, then the economy tanked. As Chrysler battled cratering demand and fought to keep the company out of bankruptcy, the entire Magnum lineup was thrown overboard, making the 2008 models the last.

◀ *2009 DODGE*
CHALLENGER R/T

The Challenger line expanded for 2009, with base SE (3.5-liter V-6; 250 horsepower with mandatory automatic transmission) and performance-oriented R/T (5.7-liter Hemi V-8; 372 horses with automatic or 376 with the newly available six-speed manual) joining top-dog SRT8 (6.1-liter V-8; 425 ponies with automatic or manual). Mopar fans rejoiced. Both performance Challengers were swift, but rather hefty; the SRT8 weighed in at more than 4100 pounds.

▶ *2009 DODGE*
CHARGER SRT8

Charger continued into 2009 with few changes. The SRT8 priced from $38,970. The unthinkable happened on April 30, 2009, when Chrysler and about two-dozen subsidiaries filed for bankruptcy protection in federal court. On June 10, the company's ongoing operations were transferred to a new entity—"Chrysler Group LLC"—via financing provided by the U.S. and Canadian governments. As part of the deal, Italian automaker Fiat was given management control of Chrysler, along with an ownership stake.

◀ *2010 DODGE*
CHALLENGER R/T CLASSIC & SRT8

To commemorate Challenger's 40th Anniversary, Dodge released the Furious Fuchsia Challenger for 2010, both in R/T Classic (left) and SRT8 (right) trim. SRT8s were limited to just 400 examples and sported kitschy Pearl White leather seats, chrome exhaust tips, 20-inch SRT forged aluminum wheels with satin black accents, and a serialized dash plaque. Dodge's limited-edition Challenger colors effectively revived the spirit of the fondly remembered "High Impact" Mopar hues of the early 1970s.

▶ *2010 DODGE*
CHALLENGER DRIFT CAR

Detroit's modern-day muscle cars found a whole new venue for competition when the popularity of drifting took off in the United States in the 2000s. Born on Japanese mountain roads, drifting evolved into a full-fledged motorsport where drivers intentionally induce oversteer but maintain control of the car. Drifting competitors are judged not on elapsed time, but on "style points" such as slip angle, tire smoke, corner entry and exit speed, and crowd reaction. Two-time Formula Drift (FD) champion and Hollywood stunt driver Samuel Hübinette drove a carbon-fiber-bodied 2010 Challenger during that year's international drift-race season. Here, Hübinette negotiates a curve at Long Beach.

◀ *2010 DODGE*
MOPAR '10 CHALLENGER

The 2010 Mopar '10 Challenger was a 500-unit limited run. Body color was restricted to Brilliant Black, with Mopar Blue, Red, or Silver as available accent colors. More accents: 20-inch forged gloss-black wheels and a dramatic black-chrome grille. A cold-air intake fed the 5.7-liter Hemi that was good for 379 horsepower and 410 pound-feet of torque. Automatic transmission versions of Mopar '10 came with a T-handle shifter; manuals had a pistol grip. Suggested retail was $38,000, and the manual added another $1000.

◄ *2011 DODGE*
CHALLENGER DRAG PAK

Dodge offered the 2011 Mopar V-10 Challenger Drag Pak to factory-approved drag racers for competition in NHRA Stock Eliminator and Super Stock classes. Equipment included competition wheels and tires, solid rear axle with performance gear ratio, a two-speed drag-race transmission, competition fuel system with fuel cell, and an interior-gauge package. The basic Challenger body was modified for race duty. There was no windshield wiper assembly, no air conditioning, no heater, no rear seats, and no power steering. The floor was modified for transmission and solid rear axle clearance. Door windows were polycarbonate plastic, and there were many other changes that made the car unsuitable for street use. White paint was standard, and the price was $85,512. Three options were available. A $7950 Competition Package added an eight-point roll cage, safety harness, and mesh window net. A range of body colors other than the standard white were available for a hefty $6800. And finally, a Mopar-logo body wrap cost $950.

2011 DODGE
CHALLENGER 392 SRT8

The top-dog production Challenger was renamed 392 SRT8 for 2011, in recognition of its new 6.4-liter V-8—close enough to 392 cubes for Dodge to evoke the heritage of the original 1957-58 Chrysler 392 Hemi. The 2011 mill put out 470 horsepower and 470 pound-feet of torque. A special run of 1492 Inaugural Edition models like this one got unique interior trim and a choice of two paint schemes: Deep Water Blue with Stone White stripes or Bright White with Viper Blue stripes.

◄ *2011 DODGE*
CHARGER R/T

Dodge Chargers were seriously reworked for 2011 with aggressive new bodywork and a redesigned interior. All R/Ts packed a 5.7-liter Hemi and 370 horsepower. R/Ts with the Road and Track Package got a blacked-out grille with a "heritage" R/T badge, among other tweaks.

► *2011 DODGE*
CHARGER REDLINE

Even before the 2011 Charger went on sale, Dodge displayed a one-off "Redline" show car at the 2010 Specialty Equipment Market Association (SEMA) show in Las Vegas. Based on the R/T with its 5.7-liter Hemi, Redline added a unique aluminum hood, lowered suspension, and 22-inch wheels and tires. The Hemi was hopped up with a cold-air intake, headers, and specially tuned exhaust. The exterior was given a blacked-out look with a black roof, front lower and rear-end treatments, and carbon-fiber mirror caps. Black side scoops on the front doors were reminiscent of the scoops on the 1970 Charger R/T. Smoke-tinted headlights and taillamps provided further contrast with the Redline Red paint.

◄ *2011 DODGE*
MOPAR '11 CHARGER

Unlike the show-car-only Redline, Dodge offered 1000 production copies of the limited-edition Mopar '11 Charger. Powered by the 5.7-liter Hemi, the specially equipped Charger featured larger-diameter stabilizer bars, along with front and rear shock-tower braces for improved handling. The exterior was finished in Pitch Black paint with Mopar Blue racing stripes. Specific-design 20-inch "Envy" alloy wheels were finished in gloss black and fitted with Goodyear F1 Supercar skins. Interior enhancements included unique leather seats with Mopar Blue stitch detail, engine-turned instrument panel, and a special identification plaque. Mopar badges on the grille and rear deck marked the outside. Buyers of the $39,750 car also received a special box with production information and the car's build date.

▼ *2012 CHRYSLER*
300 SRT8

Chrysler redesigned the 300 sedan for 2011, but the high-performance SRT8 variant arrived for 2012. It ran the 6.4 liter Hemi with 470 horsepower backed by a 5-speed automatic. Big Brembo brakes kept the Hemi's muscle in check. A lowered suspension, specific front fascia, and 20-inch wheels helped SRT8 look meaner than lesser 300s. This car wears the available Black Chrome Package that added a dark finish to the grille, rear valance, and wheels.

▲ *2012 DODGE*
CHARGER SRT8

After a short hiatus for the 2011 model year, the SRT8 version of the Charger was revived for 2012. It got a 470-horsepower version of the 6.4-liter Hemi from the Challenger 392 SRT8, plus exclusive 20-inch wheels and various styling touches that gave it an even more aggressive look than "regular" Chargers.

▲ *2012 CHRYSLER*
MOPAR '12 300

To help Mopar mark its 75th Anniversary, Chrysler announced a limited-edition Mopar '12 edition of the Chrysler 300. Scoot was provided by the 5.7 Hemi with 363 horsepower, and curves were handled with a stiffer "track-tuned" suspension. Black-chrome trim, Gloss Black paint, and other blackened trim marked the exterior along with Mopar Blue highlights. The same formula was followed inside. Announced production was 500 units.

▼ *2012 DODGE*
CHARGER SRT8

Charger SRT8's mandatory five-speed automatic transmission included steering-wheel shift paddles for manual gear changes, and a driver-selectable two-mode adaptive suspension was standard. Dodge announced the 2012 Charger SRT8 could run 0-60 mph in the high 4-second range, cover the quarter mile in the high 12s, and go from 0 to 100 mph and back to 0 in less than 16 seconds. Top speed was 175 mph.

2012 DODGE
CHARGER SRT8 SUPER BEE & CHALLENGER SRT8 392 YELLOW JACKET

Dodge also reprised the Charger SRT8 Super Bee for 2012. Available in either Stinger Yellow or Pitch Black, the exterior featured Super Bee graphics on the rear fenders and unique 20-inch wheels. The black interior featured Super Bee-specific cloth performance seats with yellow-and-silver striping, silver stitch detailing, and embroidered Super Bee logos. Mechanically, it followed the SRT8 with the 470-horse 6.4-liter Hemi and automatic. Meanwhile, 2012 Challenger SRT8 392s could be equipped with a limited-edition "Yellow Jacket" appearance package (background).

▶ 2012 DODGE
CHALLENGER SRT8 ACR

At the 2011 SEMA show in Las Vegas, Dodge showed a modified Challenger SRT8 ACR. ACR is the acronym for American Club Racing; the moniker was first used on special versions of the 1995 Dodge and Plymouth Neons aimed at grassroots racers. It later appeared on the Dodge Viper. The one-off SEMA Challenger ACR was equipped with several parts available through Mopar, including a coil-over suspension, front and rear shock-tower braces, and a short-throw shifter. The exterior was finished similar to the Viper SRT10 ACR, with a white body, charcoal painted roof, and an offset red stripe.

THE FUTURE

Today's muscle Mopars will surely be sought-after collector cars tomorrow, so it's ironic that their seeds were sown during Chrysler's fraught 10-year partnership with Mercedes-Benz parent Daimler AG. Far from the "merger of equals" it was claimed to be, DaimlerChrysler amounted to a German takeover, and Chrysler suffered for it in many ways. To no one's surprise, the troubled "marriage" ended in divorce during 2007, just before the U.S. economy began spiraling down into its worst recession since the 1930s. A much-weakened Chrysler then fell into the hands of Cerberus Capital Management, a "strip and flip" private-equity firm that seemed intent on killing the proud automaker for the sake of "rescuing" it.

Finally, in 2009, the U.S. government forced Chrysler to reorganize under Chapter 11 protection in exchange for loans that the company desperately needed just to keep the lights on. By design, this so-called "managed" bankruptcy was a fast-track process, and it proved controversial among those believing that such government assistance was an underserved bailout that wasted taxpayer money. (The issue was still hotly debated during the 2012 Presidential race that was lumbering along as this book went to press.)

But the dark days in bankruptcy brought hope for a bright new future in the form of Sergio Marchionne, the CEO of Italy's Fiat Auto Group. A dynamic executive who attended university in Canada, Marchionne was widely credited with Fiat's impressive turnaround in the early 2000s. In Chrysler he saw a chance to create a new automotive superpower with the global scale and earnings potential to rival the successful Franco-Japanese Renault-Nissan alliance under Carlos Ghosn. No less important to Mopar muscle fans, Marchionne was a "car guy" with a deep understanding of the North American market—and a tireless workaholic.

Marchionne was soon named CEO of Chrysler as well, and moved swiftly to unify the two automakers' operations and product planning. At the same time, he began to repair the wreckage of the DaimlerChrysler and Cerberus eras while backing important new Chrysler products with both resources and his personal encouragement. By early 2012, Chrysler had not only paid back its government loans, it was making real money again after scoring 24 consecutive months of higher year-on-year sales, helped by the well-received new 2011 Jeep Grand Cherokee and refurbished 2011 Chrysler 300 and Dodge Charger.

With all this, Chrysler's near-term fortunes will obviously be intertwined with Fiat's. What will that mean for Mopar muscle? Primarily it means that Chrysler is again strong enough to stay in the high-performance business, competing toe-to-toe with Ford and General Motors in the great Detroit tradition. Of necessity, however, the cars will be rather different, reimagined in light of fast-rising

Thom Taylor envisions a possible revived 'Cuda as a new-age re-do of the second-gen 1967-69 Barra-cuda, with swept-back features and a rakish fastback roofline.

fuel-economy standards and the ongoing environmental concerns of many lawmakers and car buyers. The same will apply to the next-generation Chevrolet Camaro and Ford Mustang.

So what can we expect in Chrysler's coming muscle cars? Though we're light on specifics at this point, we can make some general educated guesses based on clues from the rumor mill and Chrysler itself.

For starters, it's reported that Chrysler and Fiat are jointly developing a new rear-wheel-drive platform that would likely host the next Chrysler 300 and Dodge Charger, as well as an expected replacement for the top-line Alfa Romeo 159 at Fiat's upscale sporty brand. All these would be midsize sedans that are smaller and lighter than today's LY-platform 300/Charger. A new Mustang/Camaro fighter could also utilize this architecture, perhaps cut down a bit…but it may not be a new Dodge Challenger.

Which brings up clue number 2. We understand that Chrysler has registered—or maybe re-registered—"'Cuda" as a trademark name. This suggests a revival of the original Challenger's Plymouth compatriot of the early 1970s, except that this new 'Cuda might be modeled on the handsome 1967-69 Barra-

cuda fastback coupe instead of the 1970-74 E-body that inspired today's Challenger. Noted designer and automotive artist Thom Taylor has illustrated how such a car might look in slightly exaggerated "early thoughts" form. Tone this down a bit and you'd have an eye-popping production design that's as retro as the current Challenger, yet still 21st-century fresh and, no less important, decidedly different from what Chevy and Ford are known to be planning. Likewise the interior, which Thom projects as a deft blend of four-dial E-body gauge cluster and a contemporary center stack with ample space for today's obligatory infotainment touchscreen. A pistol-grip shifter is pure nostalgia, but would feel just as "right" as ever, not to mention working equally well with manual or automatic transmission. Hey, you just can't improve on some things, and this is one of them.

Now to clues number 3 and 4. Chrysler is moving to market its hottest wares with the SRT (Street and Racing Technology) badge, starting with the redesigned 2013 Viper. Some see this as needless branding mumbo-jumbo, but it's very convenient for a new 'Cuda, as Chrysler isn't about to resurrect the Plymouth nameplate after more than a decade. Now, it so happens that the head of Chrys-

ler's in-house performance division is also the company's design chief, the talented and affable Ralph Gilles (pronounced "Zheels"). It's reported that Gilles has long wanted to do a new Barracuda, thus adding credence to speculation that the Challenger will step aside for an SRT 'Cuda.

Whatever its name and appearance, Chrysler's new-wave ponycar is almost sure to use smaller, more fuel-efficient engines than the current Challenger. We see at least two. The big gun would be a Hemi V-8 downsized to 5.0-5.5 liters and running twin turbochargers, which should allow matching or besting the 470 horsepower of today's 6.4-liter "392." The likely addition of Fiat's innovative Multi-Air valve-control system would improve both mpg and emissions performance. The other choice could be a twin-turbo, MultiAir version of Chrysler's excellent 3.6 Pentastar V-6,

tuned to approximate the 5.7 Hemi's current 372/376 horsepower. We can also imagine the V-6 getting a new cylinder head with hemispherical combustion chambers as a kind of junior Hemi. Transmissions? What else but a 6-speed manual and Chrysler's new 8-speed automatic option?

As for the rest of it, logic suggests a new 'Cuda/Challenger will offer most all the performance, safety, comfort and convenience features available for today's Dodge ponycar. Possible additions include a multi-mode adaptive suspension and, for weekend racers, special-order "Track Paks" with a raft of upgraded components and tire-shredding super-short axle ratios.

When can we expect to see this car? That's hard to say, but the next-gen Camaro and Mustang are due for 2015, and Chrysler is surely aware of that. Need we say more?

FORD MOTOR COMPANY

H enry Ford brought affordable V-8 power to the masses in 1932 with the landmark "flathead" V-8. The spunky 221-cid engine was rated at an impressive-for-the-day 65 horsepower, and it responded exceptionally well to performance modifications. When the Mercury brand debuted for 1939, Ford's new upscale siblings all carried a 95-hp 239.4-cid flathead that was even more popular with hot rodders than the original. The flathead helped spawn an entire speed-parts indus-try, and with it a high-performance culture that eventually led to the birth of the muscle car.

The flathead lasted all the way until 1954, when Ford's first modern overhead-valve V-8, the 130-hp, 239-cid "Y-block," arrived. As the Fifties horsepower race accelerated, the Y-block received several displacement increases, topping out at 312 cubic inches by '56. An available McCulloch supercharger pushed the 312's hp rating to 300 for '57, but few Fords were so equipped. Though the flathead had reigned supreme in hot-rod circles, the Y-block didn't enjoy the same popularity...especially after 1955, when the fabulous Chevy "small-block" V-8 stole the show.

Ford's "big-block" FE-series V-8s were introduced for 1958, with the top 352-cubic-inch version rated at 300 horsepower. By 1960, the best 352 was putting out 360 horsepower, and Ford further tweaked the FE into a 401-horsepower triple-carb 390 for 1961. This escalated to 406 cubes and 405 horsepower in '62, and a thundering 425-horsepower 427 during 1963.

Ford Galaxies were formidable competitors on NASCAR's superspeed-ways in the early Sixties, especially after picking up a more aerodynamic "semi-fastback" roofline in 1963½. They were less successful at the drags, where the 427-powered big Fords had to contend with quicker, lighter rivals. Ford built a batch of special lightweight racing Galaxies during '63, but still had trouble with the best Mopars and Pontiacs at the strip.

Meanwhile, the Mercury division continued in its role as Ford's upmarket sibling. Though Mercurys boasted their own distinct styling and classier trimmings, their underpinnings and engines were shared

with Ford. Mercury's version of the new-for-'63 427 was called "Super Marauder"; with it came a strong performance/racing theme in Mercury's marketing.

Another run of lightweight drag Galaxies was built for 1964, but when those still came up short at the drags, Ford took drastic measures. By shoehorning its hottest "high-riser" 427s in a limited run of its midsize Fairlane two-doors, Ford created the Thunderbolt, which earned Ford the '64 NHRA Manufacturer's Cup. Mercury followed the same formula with a handful of purpose-built 427 Comets.

Ford had an immediate runaway hit on its hands with introduction of the Mustang in 1964. Though it was a youth-market home run and could be fitted with a snappy 289-cid small-block V-8, the Mustang wasn't a true muscle car at the start. But hotter steeds were soon to follow. Ford partnered with Carroll Shelby to create the hard-edged 1965 Shelby GT-350 Mustang, kicking off a partnership that would last the rest of the decade, and big-block 390 power was added to the mainstream Mustang lineup for 1967. Mustang also gained an upmarket cousin for '67 in the luxury-sport Mercury Cougar.

Ford's first fully realized muscle intermediates, the Ford Fairlane 500 GT and Mercury Comet Cyclone GT, arrived for 1966 and continued for '67 with minor styling changes. They sported all the expected hot-car styling tricks, but their 335-hp 390s didn't have the suds to compete with a Hemi or GM's big blocks on the street. A streetable 427 was available for non-GT Fairlanes, but it was expensive and very rare.

Though Ford enjoyed high-profile wins in virtually all forms of big-league international racing, its victories at the track didn't translate to supremacy on the street, where the real muscle-car pecking order was established. That changed in April 1968, when the 428 Cobra Jet engine was unleashed. Finally, here was an engine that could easily hang with the best from GM and Mopar. The first 50 went into lightweight Mustang fastbacks to make them legal for NHRA drag racing, and eight of them went on to dominate the Super Stock class at the 1968 Winternationals. The 428CJ became a mid-'68 option in Mustangs and Torinos and their Mercury Cougar and Cyclone cousins.

With the introduction of the sleek, fastback-bodied Ford Torino and Mercury Cyclone for 1968, Ford had an especially effective weapon for NASCAR's superspeedways. The Torino/Cyclone duo boasted such an aerodynamic advantage

on the high-banked big-oval tracks that Dodge conjured up a special run of slicked-up Charger 500 models for 1969, which started the Ford/Chrysler "aero wars." Ford fought back with the droop-snoot '69 Torino Talladega and Mercury Cyclone Spoiler II.

Ford also answered Plymouth's budget-friendly 1968 Road Runner with the new-for-'69 Fairlane Cobra, which packed the Cobra Jet 428 as standard equipment. The '69 Mustang lineup added no less than three new performance models: the Boss 302 (Ford's response to the Camaro Z/28), Boss 429 (built so Ford could qualify its radical new "shotgun" Boss 429 engine for NASCAR racing), and the Mach 1 (a muscled-up fastback with stripes, a flat-black hood, and an available "shaker" hood scoop). The Mercury Cougar picked up some extra flash with the introduction of the Eliminator model, which was tricked out along the lines of the Mustang Mach 1 and could be had with 351, 390, 428CJ, or Boss 302 engines.

For 1970, Ford Torinos and Mercury Cyclones got swoopy new styling and a new performance engine, the 370-horsepower 429 Cobra Jet. Mustang was redesigned on a larger, heavier platform for 1971; the Boss 302 and Boss 429 were replaced with a single Boss 351 model with 330 horsepower, and the "non-Boss" 429 was still available in both the Mustang and Torino/Cyclone.

Like Chrysler and GM, Ford retreated from the muscle-car business after '71, and began focusing on the burgeoning "personal-luxury" market instead. The 429 fell off the Mustang's options list for 1972, although it was still available in the redesigned Gran Torino Sport in low-compression form. By 1974, names such as Brougham and Elite had replaced Cobra and GT in the Torino model lineup.

Likewise, Ford's ponycar completely changed course for 1974 with the introduction of the Mustang II. Drastically downsized from the previous generation, the Mustang II was based on a new platform that was shared with Ford's Pinto subcompact. Performance fans were no doubt disappointed at the lack of a V-8, but the Mustang II's strong sales proved it was the right car for the times. The Mach 1 was still around in name, if not in spirit; its main talking points were a standard 171-cube V-6, white-letter tires, and flat-black paint accents. In 1975, the 302 V-8 returned, but it topped out at a meager 139 horsepower. The Mustang II's appearance got more aggressive with the ostentatious 1976-78 Cobra II and

'78 King Cobra, but its actual performance didn't; the 139-hp 302 remained the top engine option.

An all-new "Fox-body" Mustang arrived in 1979, with a 140-horse 302 as the top engine option. Mercury got its own version called Capri, which lasted through 1986. The raciest '79 Mustangs were those equipped with the Cobra package, which could be had with the 302 or a 131-hp turbocharged 2.3-liter four-cylinder. A revived Mustang GT replaced the Cobra in 1982, packing a hotter 5.0 and a mandatory four-speed manual transmission. At 157 horsepower, it wasn't truly muscular by Sixties standards, but it was a good start . . . and Ford would continue to feed the Mustang more oats as the Eighties progressed. By 1987, the turbo four had been phased out, and the 5.0 was fuel-injected and putting out 225 hp.

By the dawn of the Nineties, the Mustang had become a true darling of the high-performance aftermarket. The 5.0 engine was remarkably responsive to simple modifications and speed parts, and the Fox chassis/suspension, while never on the cutting edge of automotive technology, offered a sturdy platform for a wide variety of drag-racing or corner-carving upgrades. Their modification-friendly nature also made Mustangs popular with aftermarket tuners. Companies such as Steeda Autosports, Saleen Autosport, and Roush Performance produced a wide variety of Mustang parts, plus turn-key modified Mustangs that were spiritual successors to the 1960s Shelby GT-350s and GT-500s.

With a redesigned 1994 model on the way, Ford gave the long-serving Fox Mustang a fitting farewell with the "factory-tuned" 1993 SVT Cobra. The new '94 'Stangs boasted fresh styling with several nostalgic touches from Mustang's past, along with a regular-production SVT Cobra model. In 1996, the trusty old 5.0 V-8 was finally put out to pasture in favor of a more up-to-date 4.6-liter modular ohc V-8.

More nostalgia was on the way as the 2000s arrived. Ford paid homage to one of history's best-loved Mustangs in 2001, with a specially equipped Bullitt model that was decked out like Steve McQueen's classic '68 fastback in the movie of the same name. The Mach 1 name returned as a limited-edition model in 2003, complete with a throwback "Shaker" hood scoop just like the original Mach 1's.

Mercury dusted off a performance name from its past and made one last stab at the muscle market for 2003. Based on the rear-drive Grand Marquis sedan, the Mercury Marauder attempted to follow the 1994-96 Chevy Impala SS play-

book with black paint, a strong V-8, and a mean attitude. It didn't even match the seven-year-old Impala's acceleration, however, and it lasted only two years. (The entire Mercury division lasted only seven more years; the brand was discontinued after a short run of 2011 models.)

A landmark "retro" redesign for 2005 brought classic Sixties styling cues to the Mustang—and showed that Ford was still committed to its ponycar even after GM had abandoned the Camaro and Firebird. The new car was a home run with both critics and the buying public. The classic Shelby GT500 nameplate made a heroic return as a 2007 model, boasting 500 horsepower from its supercharged 5.4-liter engine. The Bullitt coupe got a welcome reprise in 2008 and 2009.

The redesigned, reinvigorated Mustang enjoyed a few years with no direct competition, but that changed with the rebirth of the Dodge Challenger for 2008 and the Chevrolet Camaro for 2010. Mustang's resurrected rivals undoubtedly spurred Ford to keep the Mustang competitive; a thoroughly refreshed Mustang arrived for 2010. Exterior styling was updated, interior materials were vastly improved, and the Shelby GT500 gained another 40 horsepower, for 540 total. For 2011, GTs got an outstanding new 412-hp 5.0-liter V-8, and the Shelby GT500 was bumped up to 550 hp. The next year, Ford revived the hallowed Boss 302 moniker on a car that was truly worthy of the name. With a 444-hp variant of the new 5.0 and a full track-tuned suspension, the 2012 Boss 302 was far beyond a mere nostalgic stripes-and-spoilers package.

With Camaro now outselling Mustang, Ford gave its 2013 ponycars another freshening in early 2012. Changes included a mild facelift, eight more horses for the GT's V-8, a manual-shift function for the optional automatic transmission, and a Track Package that upgraded stick-shift GTs with various Boss 302 components. Also newly available were genuine Recaro seats and a "Track Apps" data display showing acceleration times, lateral g-forces, and braking performance.

Hard on those hooftracks came a 2013 Shelby GT500 that packed a supercharged 5.8-liter V-8 with an astonishing 662 horsepower to decisively out-muscle Camaro's new ZL1 models. Chassis components were suitably upgraded to cope with the extra 112 horses and a potential 200-mph-plus top speed. It's hard to imagine that the amazing 2013 GT500 could be topped, but given Ford's incredible new-product surge over the past few years, anything is possible.

▼ *1962 FORD*

GALAXIE

Ford answered Chevy's 409 and Mopar's "Max Wedge" 413 with its first 400-plus-cubic-inch V-8. Delivered partway through the 1962 model year, Ford's 406 was basically a bored-out variant of the 390. Called the Thunderbird 406 High-Performance V-8, but available only in the Galaxie, it signaled a fresh performance push from the folks in Dearborn. The 406 was only available with a 4-speed manual transmission and 15-inch tires. Breathing through a single Holley four-barrel carb (shown) it was rated at 385 horsepower.

▲ *1962 FORD*

SUNLINER WITH STARLIFT ROOF

The 1960 and '61 Ford Starliner coupes had slippery rooflines that worked great on the nation's stock-car tracks, but Ford switched to boxy Thunderbird-inspired roof lines for the 1962 Galaxie two-doors. In an attempt to improve the car's fortunes on the track, Ford tried to sneak a bolt-on "Starlift" top for the Sunliner convertible past NASCAR rule makers. It brought back the Starliner's racy lines, but race officials only allowed the Starlift to run in a single race.

▼ *1963½ FORD*

GALAXIE 500/XL

Galaxie two-doors started 1963 with an unaerodynamic notchback roof that many call the "box top." In February 1963, Ford introduced this slanted rear roofline for the "1963½" Galaxie 500 and 500/XL (shown). Called the Sports Hardtop, the semi-fastback was two inches lower than the notchback and allowed a great aerodynamic advantage on NASCAR superspeedways.

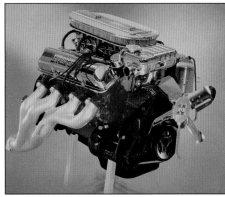

▲ *FORD*

427 ENGINE

During '63, the 406 was replaced by a new 427, which was basically a 406 bored by .010 inch. Though called a 427, the engine actually ran a 425-cubic-inch displacement. The 427 also got significant improvements over a 406, including a forged crankshaft, cross-bolted main-bearing caps, forged aluminum pistons, and an aluminum intake. The strongest 427 was the "R-code" version that used a pair of four-barrel Holleys for 425 horsepower.

1963½ FORD
GALAXIE 500

When the Sports Hardtop debuted, the hottest engines were still 406s, but the 427 arrived soon thereafter. As with the 406, 427s only came backed by a four-speed manual transmission. Galaxie 500s had a bold bi-level side chrome treatment, seven hash marks on each rear fender, and a rear panel that reprised the front grille design. Inside, there was the redesigned instrument panel shared by all '63 full-size Fords. The 500 had a front bench seat; 500/XLs used front buckets and a console instead. Despite its late arrival, 134,370 copies of the Sports Hardtop were produced (including 100,500 as Galaxie 500s) to 79,446 of the notchback hardtops.

▼ 1963½ FORD
GALAXIE 500

While the 1963½ Ford Galaxie's racing exploits in America are well documented, some may be surprised that it was quite competitive in overseas road racing as well. One of the best known is this Galaxie owned by London, England-based Ford dealer John Willment. Jack Sears drove the car in the 1963 British Saloon Car Championship, winning the season title.

▲ 1963½ FORD
GALAXIE 500

Ford came on strong in NASCAR for '63, with "Tiny" Lund winning the Daytona 500 in a Galaxie. In drag racing, however, the competition weighed about 3200 pounds, about 300 less than a Galaxie. Ford fought back with a run of 50 lightweight Galaxies with fiberglass front body panels and aluminum front bumpers that slashed about 174 pounds. These race-only Fords ran 12.07-second quarter miles at 118 mph, but still weren't fast enough to win any NHRA national titles. This is Dick Brannan giving it his best in one of the '63½ lightweights.

▶ *1963½ MERCURY*
MARAUDER

Mercury's counterpart to the 1963½ Galaxie Sports Hardtop was the Marauder, a new nameplate that eschewed the reverse-slant "Breezeway" roof used on other big Mercurys. Engine choices began with a 250-horsepower 390-cubic-inch V-8, but stretched to a dual-quad, solid-lifter 427 with 425 horses. Pioneer auto writer Tom McCahill said the big 427-powered Marauder "has more hair on its chest than a middle-aged yak."

▼ *1964 FORD*
FAIRLANE THUNDERBOLT

With the strong 427 burdened by too much weight in the Galaxie, the solution was obvious: Put the mill in a lighter car. The job wasn't easy, but contract-car builder Dearborn Steel Tubing was able to shoehorn the 427 into the intermediate Fairlane's engine bay. The result was a handful of race-ready and street-legal, if not exactly streetable, Thunderbolts. Bob Ford, a dealership in Dearborn, Michigan, campaigned this car for driver Len Richter.

▲ *1964 FORD*
GALAXIE 500/XL

New lower-body sculpting gave Ford's sleek Galaxie 500/XL a fresh base for its semi-fastback roofline. About 265,000 Galaxie hardtops were sold, but not many carried 427 engines. The 300-horsepower 390 four-barrel and even the 250-horse 352 four-barrel were more popular with buyers who had sporting intentions. *Motor Trend* ran a 425-horse 427 with a 4.11:1 rear axle to 60 mph in 7.4 seconds, and needed 15.4 for the quarter mile. Not great, but as the Ford ads said, with 480 pound-feet "those SuperTorque Ford engines climb hills like a homesick Swiss yodeler." Ford introduced the "Total Performance" campaign in '64 as numerous Ford products and Ford-powered racers took to circuits in North American and Europe.

◄ *1964 MERCURY*
MARAUDER

Mercury offered Marauder hardtops in all three of its 1964 series. More than 8700 mid-level Montclair two-door hardtops came off the assembly lines, 6459 of them Marauder types and the balance Breezeways. Of the Marauders, this car is just one of 42 that came equipped with the 425-horsepower 427.

◄ *1964 MERCURY*
COMET

Mercury's Comet was basically a stretched Falcon, but Ford extended the Fairlane Thunderbolt treatment to a small run of A/FX 427-powered Comet two-door hardtops and wagons. Here Ronnie Sox is in action at the 1964 Winternationals. In the finals, Sox turned an 11.49 at 123.45 mph to beat Don Nicholson's Comet wagon for the A/FX trophy.

► *1965 FORD*
CUSTOM 500

Ford's big cars were completely redesigned for 1965. Though full-size performance cars were quickly losing favor with buyers, Ford still offered the R-Code 425-horsepower 427 in its full-size machines. Production was very limited, and this mid-level Custom 500 two-door sedan may be one of only three built with the dual-quad 427. The car also wears the glass headlight covers that were standard on 427-powered full-size '65 Fords.

► 1965 FORD
GALAXIE 500

Ford dominated the 1965 NASCAR season, no doubt helped a bit when Chrysler's mighty 426 Hemi engine fell afoul of the rule makers. The big 427-powered Galaxie 500 hardtops were still Ford's stock-car racers, and when the season was over they had claimed 48 wins in 55 races. Here Dan Gurney wheels a Wood Brothers-prepared '65 Galaxie to victory in the Motor Trend 500 at Riverside International Raceway in California.

◄ 1965 FORD
SHELBY GT-350

The Mustang took the new-car world by storm when it was introduced in April 1964. By January 1965, a high-performance GT-350 variant was conceived and built at Ford's behest by Carroll Shelby of Cobra sports car fame. GT-350s featured a 306-horsepower "Cobra-tuned" V-8, track-ready chassis, and weight-saving tricks like omitting the rear seat. Bigger wheels, tires, and brakes were installed, as were bold stripes and racing seatbelts. The modifications left the GT-350s more uncivilized than many customers could handle, and the cars were pricey at $4457, which limited sales to hardcore enthusiasts. Just 562 GT-350s were built for 1965.

► 1966 FORD
GALAXIE 500 7-LITRE

Big Fords looked much the same for 1966, but in reality there were extensive sheetmetal changes. A new Galaxie 500 7-Litre convertible and hardtop (shown) were added to the line. These included a new 428 engine as standard equipment. Despite 10.5:1 compression and a big four-barrel carb, the 428 wasn't a muscle mill. Rather, it was a torquey, low-revving slogger designed for big cars growing ever heavier with the addition of more and more power accessories. Despite its heft, a 7-Litre was quite fast. *Car Life*'s automatic ran 0-60 mph in a credible 8.0 seconds. Still, 7-Litre was more of a luxury liner with a hint of sport.

FAIRLANE GT

The intermediate Fairlane was restyled for 1966. It looked completely new on the outside, but the car continued to use unitized construction that had origins in the 1960 Falcon. GTs, like this new-for-'66 Fairlane convertible, packed a standard 335-horsepower 390-cubic-inch V-8. A 355-horse version had a high-lift cam, larger Holley carb, and a low-restriction air cleaner. GTs were easily identified by their black-out grille, hood louvers, and bodyside striping. Inside, bucket seats and a console were standard.

▶ *1966 FORD*
FAIRLANE 500 427

The 1964 Thunderbolt drag car set the stage for the emergence of a streetable 427-powered version of the reskinned '66 Fairlane. The side-oiler 427 came in 410- and 425-horsepower versions. Fitting the 427 into the Fairlane required bigger front springs and relocated shock towers. Also included: a four-speed gearbox, handling package, and front disc brakes. The 427 Fairlane's lift-off fiberglass hood was held by four NASCAR-style tie-down pins and had a functional hood scoop. A production run of 50 was needed to qualify the car for NHRA's Super Stock class, and Ford is believed to have built 57 of them. Most went to professional racers.

◀ *1966 MERCURY*
COMET CYCLONE GT

As Ford Motor Company's "senior compact," the Mercury Comet started out playing big brother to the Ford Falcon. But in 1966, the Comet began sharing bodies with the Ford Fairlane and moved up into the crucial new intermediate class. There, in Cyclone GT trim—as on this hardtop—it was able to join the big-engine muscle-car wars. Cyclone GTs packed a 335-horsepower 390.

▶ *1967 FORD*

FAIRLANE 500/XL

Fairlanes wore revised trim and grilles for 1967. The 427 became a regular production option, but fewer than 200 are believed to have been built. The solid-lifter mill had 410 horsepower with a single four-barrel or 425 with dual quads. Only base, 500, and 500/XL Fairlanes could get the 427; GTs stuck with the 390. Ford switched from the Galaxie to the Fairlane for the '67 NASCAR season. Parnelli Jones' Fairlane took the checkered flag at the Riverside road race, and weeks later, Mario Andretti drove a Fairlane to his first and only NASCAR victory at the '67 Daytona 500.

▼ *1967 FORD*

SHELBY GT-500

The restyled Shelby Mustangs entered the big-block ranks with the introduction of the 1967 GT-500. It used Ford's 428-cubic-inch "Police Interceptor" V-8 rated at 360 horsepower. The 428 had an aluminum "427" medium-riser intake manifold with twin Holleys, an oval alloy air cleaner, and aluminum valve covers. A Toploader four-speed or C-6 automatic were available. *Motor Trend's* GT-500 did 0-60 mph in 6.2 seconds and the quarter in 14.52 at 101.35 mph.

▲ *1967 FORD*

FAIRLANE 500

The 427 Fairlanes were still fighting it out on the nation's drag strips, but the NHRA made them run in the Super Stock/B category, where Mopars were giving everybody a rough time. The Paul Harvey rig was one of the best 427 Fairlanes, running in the low 10.9s at 127 mph, but the Fords didn't win a single national championship.

▶ *1967 MERCURY*
COMET 202

Ford's no-excuses 427 mill became a regular production option for Mercury Comets in 1967. Mercury offered it on any two-door Comet—the Cyclone, Caliente, and Capri hardtops, and the bottom-of-the-line Comet 202 pillared coupe. The last was an interesting subject. It was half-a-foot shorter than the hardtops and 100 pounds lighter. The discreet "427" front-fender emblems are the only tip-offs that this plain-vanilla example with dog dish hubcaps and a bench seat is actually a hair-raising performance car.

▼ *1967 MERCURY*
CYCLONE GT

Though availability of the 427-cubic-inch V-8s had been discreetly announced in 1966, Mercury was more open about the big engine's presence in 1967. Even then, installations were few. Mercury sales literature indicated the 427 wasn't normally offered in Cyclone GTs, but this original GT, specially equipped for stock-class drag racing, has the 410-horsepower, single-carb 427. Among its features are working hood scoops, a trunk-mounted battery for improved weight distribution, and a Ford "top-loader" four-speed transmission.

▲ *1967 MERCURY*
COUGAR

Mercury joined the ponycar craze with the '67 Cougar, a nicely restyled variant of the Mustang hardtop with a three-inch-longer wheelbase and a greater luxury emphasis. All were V-8s ranging from a 200-horsepower two-barrel 289 to a "Marauder GT" 390 with 320 horses. Mercury recruited NASCAR crew chief Bud Moore to prepare Cougars for the SCCA Trans Am series. Here, the cars of Dan Gurney (#98) and Parnelli Jones are in the pits at Kent, Washington. It was the final race of the season, and the last appearance the factory Cougars made in Trans Am.

▶ *1968 FORD*
TORINO GT

Ford's new intermediate fastback came in Fairlane 500 form and as the new Torino and Torino GT (shown). The 335-horse 390 was briefly the top engine option, but phased in during the model year was the new 428 Cobra Jet, which was conservatively rated at 335 hp. *Motor Trend* ran its 390 GT with automatic transmission through the quarter in 15.1 seconds at 91 mph.

◀ *1968 FORD*
MUSTANG COBRA JET

Ford introduced the 428 Cobra Jet engine in the Mustang starting in April 1968. The first 50 were white, lightweight fastbacks, built to meet the NHRA's production minimum. After the initial run, 428 CJs were available in any Mustang body style. The 428 Cobra Jet was based on the staid 428 big-car motor, but had larger valve heads and a version of the Police Interceptor intake. Strip versions ran a wilder cam than the street engine with solid lifters and even bigger valves. Both were factory rated at 335 horsepower; a more realistic figure for the drag motor was 410.

◀ *1968 FORD*
MUSTANG GT

Street Mustangs picked up big-block power in 1967 when the 335-horsepower 390 was added to the GT's options list. The '68 GTs got revised grilles and trim, plus "C-stripes" that wrapped around the bodyside coves. Steve McQueen thrashed a Highland Green GT through the streets of San Francisco in the motion picture *Bullitt.* McQueen's mount for one of the greatest car-chase scenes ever was modified with American Racing Torq-Thrust mags, removed trim, and a beefed-up engine and suspension. The car pictured here is a modern-day replica.

▶ *1968 FORD*

SHELBY GT-500KR

Carroll Shelby's Mustangs returned for 1968 with fastback and convertible body styles in small-block GT-350 guise and in big-inch GT-500 trim. Though Shelby Mustangs still looked wilder than Ford's ponies, they were fast becoming less special. For '68, Ford shifted Shelby production from Carroll Shelby's Los Angeles plant to Livonia, Michigan (not far from Dearborn), where contractor A. O. Smith carried out the conversions.

▼ *1968 MERCURY*

CYCLONE GT

Cyclone was Mercury's performance line for '68, listing notchback and new fastback hardtop coupes in two flavors. Standard equipment for Cyclones was the new 302-cubic-inch small-block V-8 and a fairly modest 210 horsepower. All Cyclones could be ordered with a big 335-horse 390, the mighty 427, or the new 428 Cobra Jet. Of the 13,638 Cyclones built for the model year, just 334 were GT notchbacks like the one seen here.

▲ *1968 FORD*

SHELBY GT-500KR

All '68 Shelby Mustangs wore a revised nose with a larger, more-aggressive grille opening. As before, hood and bodyside scoops were functional, as were those on the fastback roof. Midyear, the 500s added the initials KR—for "King of the Road"—and gained a new "Cobra Jet" version of the Ford 428. The engine was advertised at 335 horsepower, but the CJ produced more like 400. A GT-500KR convertible started at a princely $4594. Only 318 were built.

▶ 1968 MERCURY

COUGAR

Capitalizing on its relationship with race driver Dan Gurney, Mercury introduced a special limited edition Cougar, the XR-7G (The "G" was for Gurney). Compared to a base Cougar (left), the XR-7G got plenty of racy dress-up bits, including Lucas fog lights, circular grille badge, hood pins, nonfunctional fiberglass hood scoop, and bullet-shaped racing mirror. Most were equipped with a sunroof as well. The early production model shown here wears Rader-brand wheels, which were quickly recalled for air leakage and cracking problems and replaced with Mercury's styled steel wheels. The hottest engine available in the XR-7G was the 428 Cobra Jet, but most got 390s.

◀ 1969 FORD

FAIRLANE COBRA

Ford jumped on the budget-muscle bandwagon with the '69 Fairlane Cobra. It was a dressed-down Torino with plain interior trim, fleet-grade hubcaps, and the 428 Cobra Jet engine. A competition suspension with staggered rear shocks, F70×14 tires on six-inch rims, and hood pins were other Cobra standards. At under $3200 with the standard four-speed, ads touted the Fairlane Cobra as "Bargain day at the muscle works," though the bottom line rose quickly as the option boxes were ticked off. Notchback coupe and SportsRoof fastbacks were available. This coupe wears optional styled wheels.

▶ 1969 FORD

FAIRLANE COBRA

Ram Air, a $133 option, was dubbed CJ-R and brought a hood scoop with a vacuum flap that opened at full throttle. It required the purchase of a tach, buckets, and wide-oval tires. Ram Air Cobras with automatic and 3.50:1 limited-slip turned a 14.04 at 100.61 mph for *Car and Driver*, and a 14.5 at 100 for *Motor Trend*. C/D said Ram Air cut the ET by .2 seconds and added 1.4 mph. Early models carried a multicolored decal of a stylized snake, fangs bared and tires trailing flames. A metal Cobra emblem replaced it on cars made later in the model year.

MUSTANG MACH 1

Mach 1 debuted for 1969 as the mainstream high-performance version of the redesigned Mustang. Two- and four-barrel 351s were offered, plus the four-barrel 390. Top options were the 428 CJ, or CJ-R with "shaker" hood. Either way, a 428 Mach 1 was the finest Mustang street racer of the era. Typical ETs were around 14 seconds at 100 mph.

▲ *1969 FORD*

TORINO TALLADEGA PROTOTYPES

The NASCAR "aero wars" heated up when Ford introduced an aerodynamically-enhanced droop-nose Torino fastback in response to Dodge's '69 Charger 500. It was dubbed Talladega, after the famed Alabama superspeedway. NASCAR required that 500 Torino Talladegas be built to qualify it as a production car: Ford made 754, including prototypes. Each had a 335-hp 428 CJ, C6 automatic, 3.25:1 Traction-Lok, and Competition Handling Suspension. The two cars pictured here are early prototypes that Ford sold to race-car builder Banjo Matthews in 1971; production Talladegas didn't have hood scoops or the Torino GT-style stripes.

1969 FORD

MUSTANG BOSS 302

Conceived to beat the Camaro Z/28 in the Sports Car Club of America's Trans-Am road-racing series, the Mustang Boss 302 debuted as a 1969 model. Ford had to make 1000 to qualify the Boss 302 as "production," but ended up turning out 1628 for the model year. Street versions were easy to spot with their matte-black trim, rear-window slats, adjustable rear airfoil, and four-inch-deep front air dam. Under the hood was a high-winding 302 V-8, which was underrated at 290 horsepower. The engine's special features included big-port "Cleveland" heads, solid lifters, aluminum high-riser manifold, dual-point ignition, forged crank, four-bolt central main-bearing caps, and an ignition cut-out to prevent accidental over-revving.

▼ 1969 FORD
MUSTANG BOSS 429

The Boss 429 was born of Ford's need to qualify its exotic new racing engine for NASCAR. But instead of putting production units in the Torinos it ran in stock-car racing, Ford offered the engines in Mustang fastbacks. It was a serious mill: four-bolt mains, a forged-steel crankshaft, and big-port, staggered-valve heads with crescent-shaped combustion chambers. A 735-cfm Holley four-barrel with ram air, and aluminum high riser, and header-type exhaust manifolds completed the engine. Ford built 857 Boss 429s for '69, at a starting price of $4798.

▼ 1969 MERCURY
CYCLONE CJ

Mercury's Cyclone CJ came with the 428 Cobra Jet, and the Ram Air version was optional. A competition handling package was included in the Cyclone CJ's $3224 base price. A Drag Pak option replaced standard 3.50:1 gears with 3.91:1 or 4.30:1, and added an engine oil cooler. Torquey and foolproof with the automatic transmission, these were fine street racers, with consistent ETs in the high 13s at 100 mph.

▲ 1969 FORD
SHELBY GT-500

The 1969 Shelbys were Ford's work, not Carroll's. The production cars were little more than a custom styling job on the new Mustang fastback and convertible. GT-350 and GT-500 versions of each returned with a fiberglass nose and a big loop bumper/grille that increased the car's overall length by three inches compared to a "regular" Mustang. Scoops sprouted everywhere, and wide reflective tape stripes ran midway along the flanks. Despite the visual brag, added weight and a continued focus on upscale trimmings helped make these the tamest Shelbys yet.

▲ 1969 MERCURY
CYCLONE SPOILER II

The Mercury Cyclone Spoiler II was identical in concept to the '69 Torino Talladega. Both employed a stretched, tapered nose and a flush-mounted grille for ideal aerodynamics at super-speedway velocities. However, the Mercury offered a bit more visual pizzazz than the Ford. Cyclone Spoilers came in two paint schemes named after Mercury's best NASCAR drivers. Dan Gurney Specials (shown) were Presidential Blue over Wimbledon White with blue vinyl interiors, while Cale Yarborough Specials sported Candyapple Red roofs and red vinyl interiors.

◄ *1969 MERCURY*
COUGAR ELIMINATOR

Cougar's performance profile was raised in April 1969 with the introduction of the new Eliminator package. A range of engines was available, from the Trans Am-inspired solid-lifter Boss 302 to the 428 Cobra Jet. In all-out acceleration, the 290-horsepower 302 was challenged by the Cougar's weight, but the 428 CJ apparently benefited from the relatively generous wheelbase. Grip was slightly better off the line than in the shorter Mustang, and ETs were every bit as good. Eliminator didn't use the shaker hood; its standard scoop was functional only when Ram Air was ordered. A blacked-out grille, side stripes, and front and rear spoilers enhanced the look, and Mercury offered Eliminator in a palette of "high-impact" blue, orange, and yellow exterior colors. More impact could be had over dealer parts counters, which offered not only headers and dual quads, but such exotic hop-ups as deep-sump oil pans and quadruple-carb Weber setups.

▼ *1970 FORD*
TORINO GT

Torino GTs were fancier than their Cobra siblings, but they could be plenty hairy too, if the right options were selected. A 302-cubic-inch V-8 and a fake hood scoop was standard, but the Cobra Jet 429 and the Ram Air shaker hood were optional. Hidden headlamps and graduated-color "Laser" bodyside stripes were optional as well. The GT was also available as Torino's only ragtop. For 1970, Ford built 58,819 GT SportsRoofs and 7675 Cobras.

▲ *1970 FORD*
TORINO COBRA

Redesigned for '70, Ford's Torino gained an inch of wheelbase and five full inches in length, making it among the largest cars in the segment. Replacing the willing 428 was a new 429-cubic-inch mill. This wasn't the Boss 429, but a fresh design. The Torino Cobra packed a 360-horsepower 429, and a 370-horse version was available. With the available shaker scoop, this engine was called the 429 Cobra Jet Ram Air, but stayed at 370 hp.

► 1970 FORD
MUSTANG MACH 1

After the major overhaul for 1969, Mustang wasn't changed all that much for '70. Designers did tidy up the face, filling the scooped areas that held the outer pair of headlights in '69 with simulated air vents and reverting to dual-beam headlamps located within the grille. The grille itself switched to thin horizontal bars. Other tweaks included shuffled ornamentation and the elimination of the bodyside scoops. The Mach 1 picked up ribbed rocker-panel appliqués, "honeycomb" back-panel trim, twist-type hood locks, and revised striping. Base price was $3271.

◄ 1970 FORD
MUSTANG MACH 1

Up front, Mach 1s had rectangular driving lights inboard of the main beams and did without the tri-color pony emblem fitted to the center of the grille on all other Mustangs. Mach 1 came standard with a 351 two-barrel; a four-barrel 351 and the 428 Cobra Jet, with or without Ram Air, were optional.

► 1970 FORD
MUSTANG MACH 1 TWISTER SPECIAL

One of the most unusual '70 Mustangs was the Twister Special, ordered by the Kansas City sales district office for Ford's traveling "Total Performance Day," held Friday, November 7, 1969. Twister Special Mustangs were based on the Mach 1 and had additional bodyside stripes and special rear-fender graphics. All 96 Twister Special Mustangs were to be 428 Cobra Jets like this one, but Ford ran low on 428s and used 351 four-barrels in some of the cars.

▼ 1970 FORD
MUSTANG BOSS 302

Boss 302 had new stripes for its second and final year. Its solid-lifter 302 got smaller valves for better drivability, but retained the 290-horsepower rating. Price was $3720. Formerly standard, the shaker hood was now optional. Rear-window louvers were available for $65, a tail spoiler for $20. *Car and Driver*'s test car with a limited-slip rear end ($43) and 3.91:1 gears ($13) ran the quarter mile in 14.9 seconds at 93.4 mph.

▲ 1970 FORD
MUSTANG BOSS 429

The exotic, limited-production Boss 429 was carried over mechanically unchanged after its 1969 debut. At $4932, the Boss 429 was the costliest non-Shelby Mustang, and part of the expense was a reworked front suspension to fit the big "semi-hemi" 429. Still, because the engine was built for high-rev superspeedway racing and not drag racing, Boss 429s were upstaged on the street by the 428 Cobra Jet. Only 505 were built for '70, the car's final year.

1970 FORD
SHELBY GT-500

The Shelby GT Mustangs reached the end of the road in 1970 after Carroll Shelby asked Ford to end production of these once-special machines. Model-year 1970 Shelbys were actually converted 1969s that were left in the system after the decision to drop the program had been made. Changes were few. Two black stripes were added to the hood, and most cars were fitted with a black front spoiler similar to the type used on the 1969 Boss 302. The final year's tally: 286 GT-500s; 350 GT-350s.

▼ 1970 MERCURY
CYCLONE GT

Like its Ford Torino cousin, the Mercury Cyclone was redone for 1970. The midsize Mercs were 3.7 inches longer and about 100 pounds heavier than their Ford counterparts. The mid-range Cyclone was the GT model. Hidden headlamps and a 250-horsepower 351 were standard, but this prototype wears a GT grille badge that didn't appear in production.

▲ 1970 MERCURY
CYCLONE SPOILER

The top performance Cyclone was the Spoiler, which was also the costliest model at $3759 to start. With 11.3:1 compression, Rochester Quadra-Jet carb, and Ram Air induction, the standard 429 CJ pumped out 370 horsepower and a stump-pulling 450 pound-feet of torque. The Spoiler flaunted two spoilers—one on the rear deck and one below the front bumper, along with special graphics. *Road Test*'s automatic with 3.50:1 Traction-Lok ran a 14.61 at 99.22.

▼ 1970 MERCURY
CYCLONE SPOILER

As with the Torino, the 1970 Cyclone received a new body and an inch-longer 117-inch wheelbase. Notably, the Cyclone didn't get the Ford's fastback SportsRoof, settling instead for a slightly more conservative semi-fastback roofline. Standard interior equipment on Spoilers included high-back bucket seats and an Instrumentation Group that featured dash-mounted gauges angled toward the driver.

▲ 1970 MERCURY
COUGAR ELIMINATOR

Cougar got a new snout, and the Eliminator package entered its second and final year. Standard Eliminator color choices consisted of Pastel Blue or Competition Orange, Yellow, Blue, Gold, and Green. (Mercury's "Competition" hues matched Ford's "Grabber" colors.) The front spoiler may have worked aerodynamically, but Eliminator's rear spoiler was purely decorative. The hood scoop was functional only with the 428 CJ.

◀ *1970 MERCURY*

COUGAR

A 300-horsepower 351 was standard on the Cougar Eliminator, with the 290-horse Boss 302 and 335-hp 428 Cobra Jet optional. Mercury dealers offered Autolite Staged Performance engine upgrade kits in three levels: Impressor, Controller, and Dominator. The Boss 429 engine was listed as a Cougar option, but only two are believed to have been installed. One was in "Fast" Eddie Schartman's drag car, seen here. Note the Lakewood "Traction Action" bars visible in front of the rear slicks. These "slapper bars" prevented excessive leaf spring flexing and helped prevent wheel hop for better traction.

▼ *1971 FORD*

MUSTANG MACH 1

Mustang was redesigned for 1971, and it was the biggest one yet: eight inches longer than the 1969-70 models, six inches wider, and some 600 pounds heavier on a new 109-inch wheelbase. Mustang's muscle mainstay remained the Mach 1, which was offered with six V-8s—the meanest being a 375-horsepower 429 Super Cobra Jet. Mach 1s wore specific ID and trim, including simple flat-face hubcaps and bright trim rings. A NACA-scooped hood, body-colored front bumper, and honeycomb grille dressed up the front end.

▲ *1971 FORD*

MUSTANG BOSS 351

Though less fiery than the Boss models it replaced, the Boss 351 fastback was the quickest, most roadable '71 in the Mustang stable. A special High-Output 351 V-8 with premium internals delivered a solid 330 horsepower through a four-speed manual transmission with Hurst shifter, good for 0-60-mph times under six seconds. Alas, hot-car demand was waning fast, and Ford fired the Boss at midseason after building only 1800.

▼ 1971 MERCURY
CYCLONE SPOILER

The Cyclone Spoiler was back for 1971 with few changes beyond new side stripes. The standard engine was a 285-horsepower 351 Cleveland. The 429 Cobra Jet was optional with 370 horsepower, and the 375-horse Super Cobra Jet was available too. Cyclone sales plummeted from 13,496 units in 1970 to just 3084 for '71. Of those, a mere 353 were Cyclone Spoilers.

▲ 1971 MERCURY
COUGAR XR-7

Markedly bigger than before, the redesigned Mercury Cougar adopted a bulkier, more formal appearance. The Eliminator option was discontinued as muscle cars were beginning to be eclipsed in popularity by luxurious coupes. In addition to chrome rocker-panel trim, the XR-7 got a half-vinyl roof. Inside, its high-back buckets had leather seating surfaces. The top engine choice was a 429-cubic-inch V-8 that cranked out 370 horses.

▶ 1972 FORD
GRAN TORINO SPORT

The redesigned Torino put on pounds and inches as it switched from unitized to body-on-frame construction. The muscle-car era was receding quickly, but the Gran Torino Sport kept up at least the appearance of performance. Sports were all V-8-powered two doors, but buyers could choose from the more traditional notchback-style hardtop shared with other Torino series, or a racy SportsRoof model (shown) that was a Sport exclusive. Both started at $3094, but the SportsRoof outsold the notchback by nearly 2-to-1.

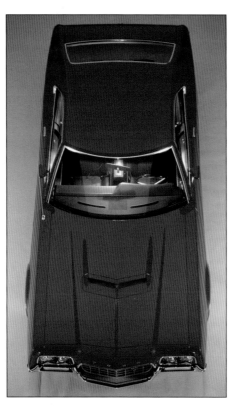

▼ 1972 FORD
GRAN TORINO SPORT

A nonfunctional hood scoop added to Gran Torino Sport's muscle car look, as did the optional bodyside striping. The base engine was a 140-horsepower 302. Four stronger V-8s were available, but only the 351 four-barrel could be mated with a four-speed manual transmission and a Hurst shifter. A 161-hp 351 two-barrel turned an ET of 17.9 at 80 mph for *Motor Trend*.

▲ 1972 MERCURY
MONTEGO GT

Midsize Mercurys were remodeled along Torino lines for 1972. Cyclone was gone with the wind, leaving a new Montego GT fastback as the "muscle" model. Base price was $3346 with the standard 302 V-8. The hottest power options included the 351 H.O. and big-block 429. Production for the year was only 5820 units. Montego GT was back for '73, but after sales fell to 4464, Mercury pulled the plug.

▼ 1973 FORD
GRAN TORINO SPORT

The federal government's "five-mph" front-bumper standard took effect for 1973, and Ford's Torino received a bulky new front end to meet the requirement. The Gran Torino Sport models continued as the performance-themed Torinos, but the rakish SportsRoof made its final appearance for '73. Optional laser stripes and Magnum 500 wheels added pizzazz, but the hottest engine in the lineup was a four-barrel 429 with just 201 horsepower.

▲ 1973 FORD
MUSTANG MACH 1

New bodyside striping and a bolder honeycomb texture on the back panel, hood scoops, and grille were the main visual differences unique to the 1973 Mach 1. The model year was the last for Mustang's optional 351, now hanging on as a Cobra Jet, with four-bolt mains, nodular iron crank, solid lifters, and dual exhausts. Net horsepower came in at 275—an impressive figure, but a far cry from the glory days of just a few years earlier. With 35,440 sold, the Mach 1 was the second-most popular 1973 Mustang.

▼ 1973 FORD
MUSTANG

Mustangs got a new grille design and front bumper for 1973. To meet new limits on oxides of nitrogen (NOx), all '73 Mustang engines received a revamped emissions-control system with positive crankcase ventilation and exhaust-gas recirculation. This base Mustang hardtop wears the Mach 1-like exterior Decor Group that cost $51. It included striping, lower bodyside accent paint, unique grille, and hubcaps with trim rings.

▶ *1976 FORD*
GRAN TORINO

Almost certainly, the "striped tomato," a red 1974 Ford Gran Torino Sport with a dramatic white stripe prominently featured in the Seventies television show *Starsky and Hutch*, has guaranteed the Gran Torino a permanent place in American pop culture. In March 1976, Ford's Chicago assembly plant began rolling out 1000 copies of the TV car that depicted its red hue and white stripe fairly accurately. Missing from the replicas, however, were the TV car's aftermarket slotted wheels, which Ford did not offer or even try to duplicate. Most owners added them, however. The Gran Torino seen here, decked out just like the TV car, is #474 of 1000, and is probably the lowest-mile example in existence.

◀ *1976 FORD*
MUSTANG II COBRA II

Purists blanched when Ford added the Shelby-like Cobra II package for 1976 Mustang II fastbacks, but the option proved quite popular—even though it did nothing for acceleration. For $325, buyers got blue racing stripes on a white body, front and rear spoilers, a nonfunctional hood scoop, rear quarter-window louvers, dual sport mirrors, styled steel wheels with trim rings, white-letter tires, special interior trim, and Cobra II emblems. This example wears upgraded aluminum "turbine" wheels.

▶ *1977 FORD*
MUSTANG II COBRA II

Cobra IIs added color choices for 1977, including this arresting black-and-gold combo that recalled the 1966 Shelby GT-350H Hertz "Rent-a-Racer." As in 1976, the standard engine in the Cobra II was the base four-cylinder, backed by a four-speed manual transmission. The V-6 was optional, but the V-8 was the most popular choice. However, customers could not buy the four-speed manual with the 302 two-barrel in the state of California, due to that state's tough emissions standards.

▶ *1978 FORD*

MUSTANG II COBRA II

Cobra IIs were little changed mechanically for 1978, but they got even flashier stripes with large "Cobra" lettering. The aggressive spoilers, louvers, and stripes certainly talked the talk, but the top Mustang II engine choice was still a two-barrel 302-cid V-8 that packed a meager 139 horsepower, so Cobra IIs didn't really walk the walk. Production of the Cobra II slumped to 8009, which was probably due in part to the introduction of the even-flashier (but no faster) King Cobra.

▲ *1978 FORD*

MUSTANG II KING COBRA

The somewhat surprising popularity of the Cobra II package prompted Ford to offer an even more outlandish stripes-and-spoilers appearance option for 1978. Though arguably over the top, the King Cobra wasn't entirely for show, as the 302 V-8, power steering, power front disc brakes, and handling-oriented suspension were included in the asking price. However, that price was $1253—about a third of the cost of a base Mustang II fastback. The King Cobra wasn't especially venomous either; it could manage 0-60 mph in about nine seconds, and the quarter mile in the mid 17-second range.

▼ *1979 FORD*

MUSTANG COBRA

An all-new Mustang bowed for 1979. Ford pushed a performance theme for the new models, but with an emphasis on handling rather than horsepower. The Mustang's available 140-hp 302 V-8 and four-speed manual transmission were good for high-16-second ETs. Prices started at $4071, and the Cobra package added $1173 to the price of a base three-door hatchback. Included were the TRX suspension and Cobra ID, but the hood decal shown on this example cost extra. Mustang's 369,936 sales for '79 nearly doubled those of '78.

▶ *1980 FORD*

MUSTANG COBRA

The racy Mustang Cobra package was updated for 1980 via a slat grille, deep front airdam, and nonfunctional reverse-facing hood scoop, all picked up from the 1979 Indy 500 Pace Car Replica. Despite the more-aggressive look, Ford replaced the 302 V-8 with a smaller 4.2-liter version, which was essentially the same engine with a lightened block and internal parts, and bore reduced to 3.68 inches from 4.00. The standard Cobra engine was still the 2.3-liter turbocharged four-cylinder; the 4.2, teamed with either four-speed manual or three-speed automatic, was optional. TRX tires continued and rode on metric-sized forged aluminum wheels.

▶ *1983 FORD*

MUSTANG GT

The 1983 Mustangs boasted a smart new "aero" face and many detail improvements, but model-year sales hit a decade low of just under 121,000. Demand soon picked up in a reviving economy where gas was plentiful and cheap. Ford called the 1983 GT "The Boss" and "One Hot Piece of American Steel"; it completely replaced the Cobra model. The '83 GT had a standard 175-hp 302 and started at $9328. *Road & Track*'s four-speed GT ran a 16.3 at 84 mph.

▲ *1982 FORD*

MUSTANG GT

Announcing Ford's sudden but welcome return to hot street cars, the 1982 GT hatchback was the quickest Mustang in years. At $8308, it was also top of the line, but its new 157-hp 302 V-8 was optional for other models at $405-$452. The hood scoop seen on the red car in this photo was a $38 option. In the background is a rare M81 McLaren Mustang, one of just a handful specially built with hopped-up turbo-four engines and IMSA-inspired body mods.

◄ *1984 FORD*
MUSTANG GT-350

Mustang marked 20 years with a modest trim option for the 1984 V-8 GT convertible (seen here with a classic 1964½ ragtop) and hatchback. Mustang traditionalists were happy to see the running-horse badge return. Finished in Oxford White with Canyon Red stripes and interior, this GT-350 package prompted a lawsuit from Carroll Shelby, who said Ford broke a promise in using the name without his permission. Ford settled. Of 5260 20th Anniversary Special GTs built in 1984, all but about 500 had the 302 HO V-8; the rest had the turbocharged four.

► *1985 FORD*
MUSTANG GT

Mustang got another nose job for 1985, this time with a simple one-slot grille above an integrated bumper/spoiler. There was extra giddyap under the hood too. Low-friction roller tappets and a high-performance camshaft muscled up the carbureted HO V-8 by an impressive 35 horsepower, to 210. Similar changes took the fuel-injected version to 180. Both 302s again teamed only with five-speed manual, which got revised gearing and a redesigned linkage. Rounding out GT improvements were beefier P225/60VR15 Goodyear "Gatorback" tires on seven-inch-wide aluminum wheels, plus gas-pressure front shocks and an extra pair of rear shocks to control axle tramp. GT interiors got articulated sport seats and an aircraft-inspired matte-gray instrument surround.

▲ *1985 MERCURY*

CAPRI RS

The Fox-body Mustang's oft-forgotten cousin was the Mercury Capri. It debuted at the same time at Ford's new-for-'79 ponycar, differing mainly in its front and rear fascia design, creased fender bulges, "bubble-back" rear hatch, and other styling details. The sportiest models were badged RS. For 1985, RS prices started at $10,232, but topped $13,000 with the high-output 210-hp V-8 and air conditioning. The Mustang-based Capri was dropped after 1986.

▲ *1987 FORD*

MUSTANG GT

For 1987, Ford styled the Mustang GT for an "increased differential" from the rest of the Mustang lineup. Opinions divided over the style merits of the GT's deep-perimeter "skirts" and "cheese grater" taillights, but most everyone liked the handsome 16-spoke 15×7-inch new wheels. A smoother new nose with flush headlamps helped lower the GT hatchback's drag coefficient to 0.38. The front end also sported an air dam with fog lights and twin air scoops.

▼ *1986 FORD*

MUSTANG LX 5.0

Mustang went to a single V-8 for 1986: a new 200-horsepower HO with electronic port fuel injection. The entry-level Mustang LX was available as a hatchback coupe or the upright-roofline notchback coupe seen in this photo. It could be had with the 5.0 HO, and many were ordered just that way. Not simply lighter and cheaper than a GT, the 5.0 LX was an interesting "sleeper" on the street because it had no stripes or badging other than the "5.0" to warn challengers that a 302 HO lurked under the hood.

▼ *1987 FORD*

MUSTANG GT

Mustang's trusty 302 V-8 was muscled up again for 1987, tacking on 25 horsepower for a total of 225. A return to freer-breathing cylinder heads and other induction changes did the trick. Torque was up as well, to a stout 300 pound-feet. An '87 GT convertible started at $15,724—almost $7700 more than a base four-cylinder notchback coupe. In the place of the GT hatchback's spoiler, GT ragtops wore a rear-deck luggage rack. All GTs got larger front disc brakes and a recalibrated suspension.

◀ *1988 FORD*

MUSTANG LX 5.0

Ford spent some $200 million on the Mustang's 1987 restyle, so no one was surprised when the '88s arrived looking exactly the same. Prices continued an upward gallop from 1987, rising another $700-$1100. LX 5.0s continued as the Mustang lineup's bang-for-the-buck leader. Producing most of its torque at fairly low rpm, the muscular 5.0-liter V-8 was well-suited for the kind of stoplight racing enjoyed by Mustang enthusiasts. The $1885 5.0-liter V-8 package brought the sticker price of an LX hatchback to $11,106. A Preferred Equipment Package including air conditioning, tinted glass, and power windows pushed the bottom line up to a still-reasonable $11,713.

1989 FORD

SALEEN MUSTANG

"Power in the Hands of a Few" was the marketing slogan for Steve Saleen's "Saleen Mustang," first built in 1984. In Shelby fashion, Saleen "race-bred" Mustangs for pure driving pleasure. Notice the Saleen Mustang racing stripes on the lower body, the front bumper molding, and the urethane air dam. The Saleen's 302 HO was stock internally, but the engine bay was reinforced with a strut-tower brace, and the exhausts were straight duals. Interior appointments included a leather-covered Momo steering wheel, a Hurst shifter, and a 170-mph speedometer. Track-worthy suspension tuning and American Racing 16-inch wheels were also part of the package.

▶ *1989 FORD*
SALEEN SSC MUSTANG

The '89 Saleen SSC (Saleen Super Car) Mustang was introduced on April 17, 1989, Mustang's exact 25th birthday. The SSC's engine mods included a revised intake plenum, enlarged throttle body, and ported heads. It packed 292 horsepower—67 more than stock—yet was street-legal in all states, quite a feat for a small company like Saleen Autosport. Special bracing in the engine and cargo bays made for a solid driving feel and more-precise handling. Saleen built only 161 SSCs in '89, all hatchbacks starting around $35,000. *Car and Driver* got a 5.9-second 0-60 run and a 14.2 ET from an '89 SSC.

▼ *1993 FORD*
MUSTANG LX 5.0

Ford attempted to spice up its aging Mustang lineup with special appearance packages for the LX 5.0-liter convertible, all with color-keyed windshield frames, exclusive color treatments, and a unique decklid spoiler. The "Yellow Package" on the 1993 LX 5.0-liter convertible cost an extra $1488 and included a white- or black-leather interior with pony-embroidered front head-rests, black floormats with running horses, a decklid spoiler in place of a rear luggage rack, and Canary Yellow paint. The long-lived Fox-body Mustang finally saw its swan-song year in 1993; a redesigned Mustang was being readied for a 1994-model-year introduction.

▲ *1991 FORD*
MUSTANG LX 5.0

By the late 1980s, V-8 Mustangs had become the dominant low-buck performance car. Changes were few from year to year, but V-8 'Stangs for 1991 got these pretty new five-spoke 16-inch alloy wheels, capped off with the traditional "pony tri-color" insignia. Despite their popularity in the performance marketplace, Mustang sales had been in decline for several years, falling from 209,769 for 1989 to 90,460 for '91. Of those, 22,018 were convertibles like this LX 5.0. It started at $19,242, about $600 cheaper than its GT ragtop sibling.

◄ *1993 FORD*
MUSTANG SVT COBRA

Loyal Mustangers got a heartening 1993 surprise in the new SVT Cobra hatchback. Conceived by Ford's two-year-old Special Vehicle Team, the Cobra packed a 235-hp 5.0 V-8 and could sprint from 0-60 in under six seconds. Starting right at $20,000, it boasted 17-inch wheels, sticky Goodyear tires, a recalibrated chassis, and unique styling touches. Exactly 4993 were built, split between 1784 in Red, 1355 in Teal, and 1854 in black. An additional 107 "R" models were built with a track-modified suspension and a pared-down interior with no back seat or air conditioning.

▼ *1993 FORD*
MUSTANG SVT COBRA

Ford stylists wisely dialed back the "boy-racer" vibe of the Mustang GT and gave the SVT Cobra a slightly more subdued, mature look. Classy taillights lifted from the departed SVO Mustang, handsome seven-blade 17-inch wheels, and an LX-style slot grille with a small running-horse emblem were a few of the styling highlights. *Road & Track* called the 1993 Cobra "the best of an aging breed," and by most any measure it was.

▲ *1994 FORD*
MUSTANG GT

A gorgeous, nostalgic redesign for 1994 thrilled Mustang fans—and Ford dealers too, for sales of the indefatigable ponycar soundly trounced those of rivals Chevy Camaro and Pontiac Firebird. Although the '94 Mustang's styling was markedly different from that of the 1979-93 design, it was built on basically the same "Fox" platform. However, the new car was more rigid and got numerous revisions aimed at increasing overall refinement. The 5.0-liter V-8 continued with little change. It was standard in the GT, but no longer available in a lower-priced model.

▶ *1994 FORD*
MUSTANG GT

The new Mustang's retro design cues included body-side scoops and tri-segmented taillights. Both coupe and convertible body styles carried over, but Mustang's hatchback was dropped because of the difficulty in building one with Ford's required levels of torsional stiffness. The LX model designation was also eliminated. This convertible wears the 16-inch five-spoke wheel standard on GTs; a 17-inch "tri-blade" six-spoke design was an extra-cost option.

◀ *1994 FORD*
MUSTANG COBRA

Ford's SVT division put together another limited-edition Mustang Cobra for mid-1994, set off by discreet Cobra fender badges, a Cobra-exclusive rear wing, unique 17×8-inch wheels, and white-faced gauges. Despite much massaging by SVT, the Cobra's 5.0 V-8 made only 240 horsepower, just 5 more than the 1993 version. *Car and Driver*'s best ET with a '94 Cobra coupe was a 14.7 at 96 mph.

▶ *1994 FORD*
SALEEN MUSTANG

Aftermarket tuners wasted no time in modifying the redesigned '94 Mustangs for better performance and looks. Saleen Autosport offered "S281" coupes and convertibles, both with a specially built 351-cubic-inch engine that put out 371 horsepower at 5100 rpm and 422 pound-feet of torque at 3500 rpm. Saleen's Racecraft-tuned suspension was standard; a Vortech supercharger was optional. Saleen claimed the S281 was capable of a 5.2-second 0-60 sprint, a quarter mile in 13.5 seconds at 105.3 mph, and 0.97g on the skidpad.

1995 FORD
MUSTANG COBRA R

For 1995, Ford offered another race-intended R version of the Cobra. The cars were immediately recognizable by their bulged fiberglass hood, fitted to clear the tall intake manifold. Also included were unique five-spoke alloy wheels with wide performance tires. Instead of the regular Cobra's 240-hp 5.0, Rs packed a 300-hp 5.8-liter V-8. The only transmission was a heavy-duty Tremec five-speed manual. The rear seat was deleted, as was the stereo and air conditioning. Top speed was 151 mph, ETs were in the low- to mid-13s. The '95 Cobra R was fully street legal, but Ford required buyers to show a current competition license from a race sanctioning body. Production was a low 252 units.

1996 FORD
MUSTANG GT

Mustang power entered the modern era for 1996 with the adoption of Ford's overhead-cam 4.6-liter modular V-8s. GTs like the one shown here ran a single-cam version with the same 215 horsepower as the last push-rod 302. Designed for future emissions standards, the new mill required extensive underhood changes to fit but was announced outside only by small front-fender badges. That year's SVT Cobras switched to a twincam 4.6 whose 305 horsepower finally brought Mustang up to performance parity with the larger-engine GM ponycars. Despite the new engine, the '96 GT was slightly slower 0-60 mph than the '95 model; the '96 did the sprint in 6.6 seconds compared to 6.1 for the '95. Quarter-mile times were identical at 14.9 seconds according to Car and Driver. Naturally, Cobras were quicker. Ford's estimated performance times for the Cobra were 0-60 mph in 5.9 seconds and the quarter mile in 14 seconds flat at 101.6 mph.

▼ 1998 FORD
MUSTANG COBRA

Mustang SVT Cobras remained visually stealthy versus the more ubiquitous GTs, but got a new five-spoke alloy wheel for 1998. Ford's Windsor, Ontario, plant built the Cobra's "mod" twin-cam V-8, whose aluminum block was cast in Italy. The crankshaft was forged in Germany. At $30,200, the Cobra ragtop (shown here) remained the priciest Mustang for 1998. While slow sales had GM pondering the discontinuation of its Camaro and Firebird models, Mustang sales for 1998 were running 30 percent above 1997 levels.

▲ 1999 FORD
MUSTANG GT

Mustang adopted Ford's "New Edge Design" theme for 1999, with fresh lower-body sheet-metal over the existing structure. The restyle imparted a crisper, slightly huskier look, with new iterations of trademark Mustang design elements such as triple taillamps and simulated bodyside scoops. A higher-lift cam, improved intake manifold, revised combustion chambers, and bigger valves added 35 horsepower to the GT's 4.6-liter V-8, for a total of 260.

1999 FORD
MUSTANG GT 35TH ANNIVERSARY

Mustang also observed its 35th anniversary in 1999. Around 4600 GTs left the factory with a celebratory 35th Anniversary Package that delivered specific wheels, trim, and leather upholstery for $2695. GTs could be distinguished from base Mustangs by the driving lights under the front bumper and the new single scoop hood (the 35th Anniversary Package added a raised hood scoop). Save for SVT Cobras, all Mustangs got a "corral" around the running-horse grille mascot and 35th Anniversary front-fender emblems. The rejuvenated '99s got a mostly thumbs-up reception. All models earned praise for melding a tighter driving feel and meatier steering with a more supple ride and less cabin noise. *Motor Trend* judged its manual GT coupe "as good or better than any stock Mustang we've ever tested...." The car dispatched 0-60 mph in 5.4 seconds, the quarter mile in 14 at 100.2 mph.

▲ *1999 FORD*

MUSTANG SVT COBRA

An updated SVT Cobra coupe and convertible bowed a few months after mainstream models, with improvements all their own. Base price was $27,470 for the coupe, $31,470 for the ragtop. New "tumbleport" cylinder heads and other tweaks lifted the twincam V-8 by 15 hp to 320, the same as the top Chevrolet Camaro/Pontiac Firebird option. However, some Cobras put out far less than the rated number, which was found to be caused by faulty intake parts. As a result, no Cobras except the R were built for 2000, and Ford repaired the '99s at no charge.

▼ *1999 FORD*

MUSTANG SVT COBRA

The big news for the 1999 Cobra was Mustang's first independent rear suspension. It consisted of high-rate coil springs, lower control arms, upper toe-control links, and a thicker anti-roll bar. All mounted to a welded-up tubular subframe along with an aluminum-case differential and Cobra-specific halfshafts. Cleverly, SVT engineered the entire setup for easy bolt-in on the assembly line. Traction control and ABS were standard on all Cobras, and were joined by big new Brembo disc brakes.

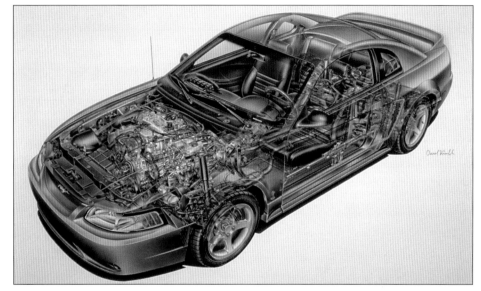

2000 FORD

MUSTANG COBRA R

For 2000, Ford offered the third of its race-bred Mustang Cobra Rs. Only 300 were built, all in red, starting at $54,995. Power came from a 385-hp 5.4-liter V-8 teamed with a beefy Tremec T-56 six-speed manual transmission. As in previous Rs, the interior had no radio, backseat, or sound deadening. However, the 2000 model included Recaro seats up front. A deep front airdam, power-bulge hood, side-exit exhaust tips, and high-flying rear wing were standard. Performance was torrid, with *Motor Trend* driving one to a 12.9-second quarter at 110.8 mph.

2001 FORD
MUSTANG BULLITT

In 2000, Ford showed a concept car com memorating the 1968 Mustang GT used in the movie *Bullitt*. For 2001, the package was put into production as the Bullitt edition for the GT coupe. It used the GT's 4.6-liter V-8, but added a freer-flowing induction system. The engine mods gave it only five hp more than the base 260-hp GT, but also provided more readily available power at lower rpms. Other enhancements included a lower ride height, Brembo front brakes, and upgraded shocks and struts. Inside were aluminum pedals, along with retro-look seat stitching and gauge faces. A total of 6500 were built, most in Dark Highland Green, though black and dark blue were also available.

◀ 2003 FORD
MUSTANG MACH 1

Ford again dipped into the nostalgia well and dusted off another classic name from Mustang's past for 2003. The reborn Mustang Mach 1 featured a novel "shaker" hood scoop that fed air to a 305-horse version of the 4.6 twin-cam V-8 from earlier SVT Cobras. Priced from $28,370, the new Mach 1 featured a firm suspension with slightly lowered ride height and Tokico shocks and struts. Also standard were the front air dam, rear spoiler, and 13-inch front brake rotors. Heritage design touches abounded. The Mach 1's 17-inch wheels recalled the design of the Magnum 500 wheels that were popular circa 1969, when the first Mach 1 was introduced. Likewise, the matte-black stripes put a new-age spin on classic muscle-car graphics. Because modern engine-management tech-nology meant that the Mach 1's engine was decidedly smoother than the big blocks of yore, the shaker scoop was mounted to a springy metal clip for more "shake."

◀ *2003 FORD*

MUSTANG SVT COBRA

Ford went all out for 2003 by supercharging the Cobra's twin-cam V-8 to create one of the most potent street Mustangs yet. With 390 horses and 390 pound-feet of torque, both the Cobra coupe and convertible could run 0-60 in well under five seconds. Larger brakes and rolling stock helped control the formidable thrust. The shifter connected to a mandatory six-speed manual gearbox. Round fog lamps and unique front and rear fascias helped distinguish Cobras from other Mustangs. A bulging twin-vent hood (to counter the blower's added heat) was also new. The Cobra coupes and convertibles were released together, at $34,750 and $38,995, respectively. Even taking into account the $1000 gas guzzler tax, Cobras were more affordable than other production cars with similar performance. *Motor Trend* timed a 2003 Cobra at 4.9 seconds 0-60 mph and 13.3 seconds at 109.58 mph in the quarter mile.

▼ *2004 FORD*

MUSTANG SVT COBRA

The 40th anniversary of the Ford Mustang heralded the end of an era, as 2004 was the final year for the Fox platform, a chassis that traced its roots all the way back to 1978. An exclusive "Mystichrome" paint option was one of the few changes for the supercharged 2004 Cobras. It was a new high-tech finish that changed hue depending on ambient light and one's vantage point. The option's $3650 price tag included chrome alloy wheels, as shown here.

▲ *2003 MERCURY*

MARAUDER

In 2001, Mercury officials announced that the Marauder, a full-size performance machine based on the Grand Marquis four-door sedan, would go on sale as a 2003 production model. With big rear-drive-sedan underpinnings and a 300-hp 4.6-liter engine, the Marauder was undeniably old school. But the excitement waned when the performance didn't live up to the hype. Production ended after two years and a mere 7608 sales. At the end of the car's run, an anonymous benefactor donated 18 Marauders to the Florida Highway Patrol.

▲ 2005 FORD
MUSTANG GT

Ford redesigned the Mustang from the ground up for 2005, effectively recommitting itself to the future of the iconic American ponycar. It was the first-ever Mustang on its own chassis; even the 1964 Mustang was based on the Ford Falcon. Clearly Ford's designers used styling cues from the popular Mustangs of the late 1960s. GT Mustangs kept the 4.6-liter V-8 from previous years, but horsepower was up 40 to 300.

▼ 2005 FORD
MUSTANG GT

Redesigned convertible Mustangs joined their coupe kin in the spring of 2005. V-8 Mustang pricing started at $25,815 for a GT Deluxe coupe and topped out at $31,420 for a GT Premium ragtop. The new Mustang was 4.4 inches longer overall than the '04, on a wheelbase stretched by 5.8 inches. Grille-mounted fog lamps, a rear spoiler, dual exhaust tips, and 17-inch wheels were GT-exclusive features. *Motor Trend* launched a GT from 0 to 60 mph in 5.1 seconds.

▶ 2006 SHELBY
GT-H

History repeated itself in 2006, when Hertz Rent-a-Car again offered a black-with-gold stripes Shelby Mustang for rental. The '06 Shelby GT-H was a true Shelby-modified Mustang, equipped with a Shelby Performance hood (with tie-down pins); a unique front fascia with a brushed-aluminum grille; and engine hop-ups such as a cold-air induction system and cat-back exhaust that boosted the 4.6-liter V-8 to 325 hp. Handling upgrades included lowering springs, a strut-tower brace, and special sway bars. The functional modifications of the GT-H became available to the general public the following year, when the 2007 Shelby GT Mustang was introduced.

◄ *2007 FORD*

SHELBY GT500

At the 2005 New York Auto Show, Ford unveiled the Shelby Cobra GT500 show car. Released in 2006 as a early 2007 model, the GT500 was the first production Ford to bear the Shelby name since 1970. It was also the most powerful Mustang yet, putting out a thumping 500 horsepower and 480 pound-feet of torque. The supercharged, 32-valve 5.4-liter V-8 had first seen duty in the 2000 SVT Cobra R, but now benefited from technology developed for the Ford GT supercar. The muscle was too much for any automatic on Ford's shelf, so the only transmission was a heavy-duty six-speed manual. Also included were a beefed-up suspension, Brembo disc brakes with 14-inch rotors up front, and sticky high-performance tires sized at 255/45ZR18 fore, 285/40ZR18 aft.

▼ 2008 FORD

MUSTANG BULLITT

Ford reprised its 2001 Bullitt-edition Mustang on the more nostalgically-appropriate body of the 2008 Mustang. A cold-air induction system boosted the 4.6 V-8 from 300 horsepower to 315, and the exhaust note was tuned to recall the sound of Lt. Bullitt's ride from 1968. Also included were a mandatory Tremec five-speed manual gearbox, tighter final-drive ratio, uprated suspension and brakes, "mag-style" wheels, and unique trim inside and out.

▲ *2007 FORD*

SHELBY GT500

The Shelby GT500's body modifications perfectly captured the spirit of the original 1967 and '68 GT-500s. The iconic Shelby stripes were standard, but the wide dorsal stripes could be deleted if the buyer desired. An aggressive front fascia, twin-vent hood, and pronounced rear spoiler capped off the look. Performance was predictably impressive. *Car and Driver* reported the best published stats: 4.5 seconds 0-60, 12.9 for the quarter mile. *Automobile* magazine accurately portrayed the new GT500 by saying it "goes fast, stops well, corners hard enough to scare dates, and should be comfortable enough to live with on a regular basis."

◀ 2008 FORD
SHELBY GT500KR

The "King of the Road" 2008 Shelby GT500KR one-upped the already brutal GT500 with a 540-horsepower version of its supercharged 5.4-liter V-8. To handle the added power, all chassis components were retuned and a front strut-tower brace installed. The carbon-fiber hood had functional scoops and vents, and it nicely recalled the hood of the original 1968 GT-500KR. Carbon-fiber was also used for the aerodynamic front splitter and even the door-mirror housings. The KR's many modifications added up to an especially steep price tag, however: Its MSRP was a whopping $79,995.

▼ 2008 FORD
MUSTANG FR500CJ COBRA JET

The '08 Mustang FR500CJ ("FR" for Ford Racing, "CJ" for Cobra Jet) was created for 2009 NHRA competition. These were purpose-built drag-racing machines that were not street-legal. Under the scooped hood was a special Cobra Jet version of the supercharged 5.4-liter V-8 that was limited to "only" 400 horsepower by race-class rules, hooked to either a six-speed manual or three-speed automatic. The '08 Cobra Jets served as a fitting tribute to the original 1968 428 Cobra Jet Mustangs that terrorized the competition at the 1968 NHRA Winternationals.

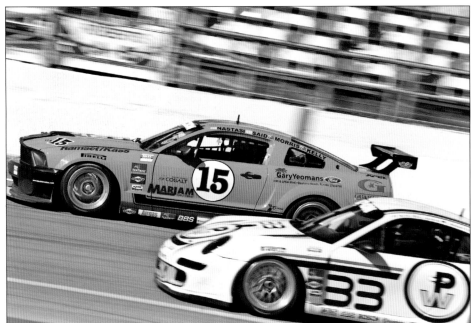

▲ 2009 FORD
MUSTANG

Mustangs remained in the thick of road-racing competition as well. Here, the #15 Black-forest Motorsports Mustang of Boris Said, Tom Nastasi, Paul Morris, and Owen Kelly dices with a Porsche 911 during the 2009 Grand Am Rolex 24 Hours at Daytona. The color scheme and #15 roundels recall Parnelli Jones' iconic 1970 Mustang Boss 302 Trans Am race car. Through its Ford Racing motorsports and high-performance parts arm, Ford offered both competition parts and turn-key, road-race-ready FR500 Mustangs to individual race teams.

◀ *2009 ROUSH*
427R MUSTANG

Livonia, Michigan-based Roush Performance turned Mustang GTs into Roush 427Rs by adding a full complement of appearance and performance upgrades. Roush offered its broad selection of aftermarket components individually, so customers could hop up their own Mustangs, or on turn-key Roush-assembled cars. The 427R was decidedly on the wild side of the scale, boasting flashy stripes, 18-inch chrome wheels, and a revamped sport suspension. The stock Mustang GT's 4.6 V-8 was bumped from 300 hp to 435 with the help of a Roush-engineered supercharger. A dealer-installed Roush exhaust system delivered a positively evil-sounding exhaust note. The car shown here retailed for $50,946.

▼ *2010 FORD*
SHELBY GT500

The Shelby GT500 was revamped for 2010 like other Mustangs. Again available in coupe and ragtop form, the 2010 GT500 got its own styling enhancements, which included such functional features as air-extractor vents on the hood and a pronounced rear spoiler for improved downforce. The supercharged 5.4-liter V-8 gained a healthy 40 hp over its 2009 predecessor, for a whopping 540 total. Convertibles like this one started at $51,325; coupes were $5000 cheaper.

▲ 2010 FORD
MUSTANG GT

The Mustang got a substantial revamp for 2010 that included restyled bodywork and vastly upgraded interior materials. The GT's standard 4.6-liter V-8 was carried over from 2009, but was upgraded with the Bullitt Mustang's "ram-air" cold-air induction system; this was good for a 15-hp boost, to 315. Ford also included fun touches such as sequential rear turn signals (á la 1960s Thunderbirds and Mercury Cougars) and an "Induction Sound Tube" that ran from the intake plenum to the cabin. Its sole purpose was to transmit the V-8's burble to the cockpit.

▶ *2010 FORD*

MUSTANG COBRA JET

For 2010, Ford again unleashed a limited run of 50 brutal, drag-race ready Cobra Jets built from its newly revamped Mustang. These turn-key race cars came from the factory with a trunk-mounted fuel cell, NHRA-certified 10-point roll cage, manual steering and brakes, and drag-race-specific shocks and springs. The all-business dash was equipped with a monster tach, and the stereo and climate controls were replaced by extra gauges and racing switchgear. The Cobra Jet shown here packs a supercharged 5.4, but naturally aspirated versions were also offered.

2011 FORD

MUSTANG GT CALIFORNIA SPECIAL

Mustang GTs were little changed on the outside for 2011, but the big news was under the hood, where an all-new 5.0-liter V-8 debuted. It was a state-of-the-art 32-valve DOHC screamer that utilized all-aluminum construction and Twin Independent Variable Camshaft Timing (or Ti-VCT). It was factory-rated at 412 hp and 390 pound-feet of torque, which blew away the 315/325 rating of the previous 4.6 V-8. Despite its outstanding power, the 5.0 was EPA-rated at 26 mpg on the highway with the six-speed manual. Shown here is a Mustang GT Premium with the nostalgic California Special package, a $1995 add-on that brought unique trim, a rear spoiler, and 19-inch wheels.

GENERAL MOTORS CORPORATION

It's often said that General Motors kicked off the 1950s Detroit "horsepower race" with its introduction of light, durable overhead-valve V-8s in the 1949 Oldsmobiles and Cadillacs. Oldsmobile's "Rocket," a 303.7-cubic-inch job, was rated at 135 horsepower, and Cadillac's 331-cube engine put out 160. Olds put its V-8 in its lightest cars to create the Rocket 88, one of the hottest cars of its day and a direct progenitor of the muscle car.

The horsepower race broke into a full gallop after Chrysler's 180-hp, 331-cid Hemi V-8 upstaged Cadillac in 1951. Of course, GM fired back—Cadillac's V-8 was bumped up to 190 horsepower in 1952, and to 210 in '53. By then, Buick had its "Nailhead" V-8, and Chevy and Pontiac received OHV V-8s for 1955.

That fabulous new 265-cubic-inch "small-block" V-8 changed Chevrolet's brand image almost overnight. The engine quickly became a favorite of racers and hot rodders, who had previously tinkered primarily with Ford's aged "flathead" V-8. In March 1955, Chevrolet began offering a 180-horse "Power Pack" version, and by 1957, the engine was enlarged to 283 cubic inches. With the new Rochester fuel-injection option, it made 283 horsepower, achieving a milestone one-horsepower-per-cubic-inch ratio.

Chevrolet issued a one-two punch for 1961, unveiling both the Super Sport package and the soon-to-be-famous 409. Essentially an upsized version of its new-for-'58 348-cid "W-head" V-8, the 409 packed 360 horsepower to start—and later versions produced up to 425. The 409 was the standard-bearer among full-size Chevys until mid-1965, when the new 396-cid "big-block" was introduced. The 396 was bored and stroked to 427 cubic inches the following year, again putting up to 425 horsepower under the hood of the Impala SS.

Pontiac received a high-performance-focused makeover similar to Chevrolet's when Semon E. "Bunkie" Knudsen took over as general manager in 1956. Bunkie ordered the removal of the traditional Silver Streak hood trim from the '57 Pontiac lineup, then introduced the flashy new Bonneville convertible. With an exclusive 370-cubic-inch fuel-injected V-8 that was good for 310 horsepower, the Bonneville was the plushest, most powerful Pontiac to that point.

The high-performance push didn't stop there. Pontiac teamed with hot-rodding legend Mickey Thompson on several of his handmade racing machines, and began attacking drag strips with special dealer-tuned "lightweight" cars soon after. The 1962 and '63 Super Duty Catalinas, with race-prepped 421-cid V-8s and aluminum front sheetmetal, were formidable quarter-mile competitors.

But the 1964 Tempest GTO was Pontiac's true breakthrough car; it was the first modern mass-production automobile to put big-cube power in a midsize body—the formula that defined the true muscle car. Pontiac circumvented a GM rule that prohibited intermediates from having V-8s of more than 330 cubic inches by making its 389-cid V-8 part of an option package for the new Tempest, a ploy that didn't require corporate approval. The GTO's smashing success prompted rival automakers to cook up their own high-performance intermediates, and the muscle-car craze officially began.

Not surprisingly, other GM divisions wanted in on the action. Oldsmobile's entry into the muscle car sweepstakes got off to a tentative start in 1964, with the F-85/Cutlass-based 4-4-2 option package. The "4-4-2" stood for four-barrel carb, four-speed, and dual exhaust, all of which were teamed with a 330-cid, 310-horsepower V-8 and heavy-duty suspension. In 1965, the 4-4-2's engine was bumped to 400 cid and 345 horses, giving the 4-4-2 numbers new meaning: 400 cubic inches, four-barrel, and dual exhaust. For 1966, standard horsepower was kicked up to 350, and Oldsmobile offered both a tri-carb option rated at 360 horsepower and a race-ready W-30 package.

Buick's muscle-market entry came midway through the 1965 model year, when the Skylark Gran Sport first appeared. Powered by the 401-cubic-inch "nailhead" V-8 (advertised at 400 cid because of GM's policy banning larger engines in intermediates), the Skylark GS sported 325 horsepower. The 401 continued for 1966, being replaced the following year by a new, thinwall-cast 400-cid V-8 producing 340 horsepower.

Chevrolet's first big-block intermediate was the limited-edition Chevelle SS 396 Z16, a mid-1965 model that packed a 375-hp 396. Only 201 were built. Things really picked up in 1966, when the SS 396 Chevelle became a separate model and more than 72,000 were sold.

At Pontiac, the GTO kept pace with its fast-expanding field of competitors by improving each year. A functional "Ram Air" hood scoop was available in 1965, and a handsome new body was rolled out for 1966. The 389 and Tri-Power option lasted through 1966, after which a larger 400-cid V-8 took over. The

1966 GTO was the most popular ever, with sales of more than 96,000 units.

GM fielded its response to Ford's hugely successful Mustang with the introduction of the 1967 Chevrolet Camaro and Pontiac Firebird. The two ponycars shared some underpinnings but boasted distinct, brand-specific styling and engine choices. Big-block power was on offer almost from the get-go, and Camaro soon added a potent Z/28 model intended to do battle with the Mustang in SCCA Trans-Am racing.

For 1968, all the GM intermediates got curvaceous new bodies on a slightly shorter wheelbase, and Chevrolet's compact Chevy II/Nova was redesigned on a platform that could accept big-block powerplants. Oldsmobile teamed up with aftermarket parts manufacturer Hurst to create the Hurst/Olds, a limited-run "executive hot rod" with a 390-horsepower, 455-cid High Output V-8, special paint and stripes, and Hurst ID.

Things got even crazier in 1969. A handful of clever high-performance Chevrolet dealers, most famously Yenko Chevrolet in Pennsylvania, bent the rules of GM's Central Office Production Order (or COPO) system to produce limited runs of fire-breathing 427-powered Camaros and Chevelles. A handful of exotic aluminum ZL-1 427-cid V-8s even made it into '69 Camaros as special orders. Meanwhile, Pontiac introduced one of the most memorable GTOs ever: the striped and spoilered Judge, with a standard Ram Air 400 rated at 366 horsepower. Pontiac also rolled out the first Firebird Trans Am for 1969, although only 697 saw the light of day.

The muscle-car era hit its peak in 1970, and nowhere was that more apparent than at General Motors. GM officially lifted its 400-cid limit on intermediate cars that year, and each division responded with 450-cube-plus monster motors.

The Buick Gran Sport was packing a new 455-cid V-8, and standard horsepower jumped to 350. The real stud in the Buick corral was the 455 Stage 1 option for the GS, which produced 360 horsepower thanks largely to a hotter cam and high-rpm valvetrain. Following in the footsteps of the GTO Judge was Buick's outlandish GSX, which broke away from the brand's traditional reserved look with front and rear spoilers, body-length stripes, and eye-searing Saturn Yellow paint. The GSX came with either the standard 455 or the Stage 1 option.

Chevelle SS power crescendoed with the availability of the solid-lifter LS6 454. The LS6's factory horsepower rating was a whopping 450, the highest ever of the original muscle-car era. Though the Hurst/Olds was the first Cutlass to receive a 455, all 4-4-2s were offered with it in 1970, and the W-30 versions were hotter than ever. The GTO got an available 455 for 1970 also, though its 360-hp rating was less than the hottest Ram Air 400s.

Midsize muscle faded quickly after 1972. Buick's Stage 1 option survived into the early Seventies, but in low-compression 270-horsepower form. The Chevelle SS lasted through '73. GTO was reduced to an option package for the compact Ventura by 1974, then mercifully retired. Surprisingly, Oldsmobile kept the 4-4-2 around through 1980, then offered the model again from 1985 to '87. However, performance dropped off quickly after 1972, leaving the 4-4-2 as little more than a sporty-looking Cutlass with better handling.

As it turned out, the Camaro and Firebird were best suited to survive the difficult performance-car climate of the 1970s. Both received a groundbreaking, European-influenced redesign for 1970, with cutting-edge bodywork that proved to be remarkably "updatable." Throughout the decade, GM's designers did an impressive job keeping the Camaro and Firebird fresh-looking and relevant to the changing marketplace. Despite some painfully lean years that very nearly led to their cancellation, the GM ponycars hung on. The second-gen Camaro and Firebird lasted through 1981, and the pair finally received a ground-up redesign for 1982.

The Eighties also saw the rise of an unlikely performance star. Buick had been experimenting with turbocharged V-6 engines since 1978, and by 1984, Regal T-Type and Grand National coupes were powered by turbo V-6s that offered surprisingly potent acceleration for the day. Both T-Types and GNs had a clean, purposeful look, but the sinister, blacked-out visage of the GN really drove the point home. A special send-off GNX model closed the line in 1987 with 276 horsepower, along with other performance and appearance upgrades. Sadly, this was the last stand for traditional rear-wheel-drive intermediate coupes at General Motors.

With that, the Camaro/Trans Am duo was left to carry the banner for affordable rear-drive performance at GM, and they would do so for the next 15 years. Most of the ponycars' performance enhancements were "trickle-down" goodies from the Chevrolet Corvette. For 1987, performance picked up, thanks to a new 225-hp tuned-port-injection engine. Camaro and Firebird were treated to another much-needed redesign for 1993. A refreshed "LT1" small-block engine was part of the deal, and horsepower was more than 300 in the Camaro SS and Ram Air Firebird by 1996.

After debuting in the 1997 Chevrolet Corvette, the completely new LS1 V-8 appeared in freshened 1998 Camaros and Firebirds. But the ponycar pair's days were numbered: Both were dropped in 2002, after years of steadily shrinking sales. GM muscle fans mourned the loss, and grieved again in 2004, when the entire Oldsmobile Division was shuttered.

With Olds gone, any hope of a resurrected 4-4-2 was dashed, but one legendary GM muscle nameplate did see a revival. The GTO made an unlikely return for 2004, as a rebadged version of GM's Australian-market Holden Commodore coupe. The LS1 5.7-liter V-8 delivered a solid 350 hp, but the GTO revival quickly fizzled when enthusiasts decided that the mildly styled new car didn't look enough like a true "Goat." Despite an upgrade to a 400-hp 6.0 V-8 for 2005, sales never took off, and the reborn GTO was killed in 2006.

Pontiac tried again with another rebadged Aussie in 2008: a large rear-drive sedan called the G8. GT versions packed a 6.0-liter V-8 with 361 horsepower. A GXP version with 415 horsepower from a 6.2-liter V-8 arrived for 2009, just as the nosediving global economy drove a nearly bankrupt GM to axe the entire Pontiac brand.

Camaro was reborn for the 2010 model year, looking nearly the same as a blockbuster concept that debuted at the 2006 Detroit Auto Show. The production cars went on sale right around the time GM filed for bankruptcy, with the company saved through emergency financing provided by the U.S. and Canadian governments. Base LS and step-up LT coupes used a strong V-6, but the top-line SS came with a 6.2-liter V-8 and as much as 426 horsepower. Convertibles arrived for 2011 in the same trim levels, and an RS appearance package was available for both body styles, just like the good old days.

The new Camaros were well received by press and public alike, and sales got a boost from the car's starring good-guy role in the *Transformers* movie trilogy. By 2012, Camaro was regularly outselling archrival Ford Mustang and far outpacing a reborn Dodge Challenger in a renewal of the 1970s "ponycar war." Though a vastly changed market held demand for all three to a fraction of yesteryear levels, muscle-car fans loved the action.

Chevrolet kept up the pressure for 2012—Camaro's 45th Anniversary year—with the ZL1. Among the many highlights of this pumped-up coupe were a rip-snorting 580-hp V-8 adapted from Cadillac's breathtaking second-generation CTS-V, a race-worthy suspension with auto-adjusting "magnetic" shock absorbers, and super-wide 20-inch tires. But hot as it was, the ZL1 was eclipsed by Ford's 662-hp 2013 Shelby GT500 Mustang, announced at about the same time.

Still, with a freshly slimmed-down, post-bankruptcy General Motors cranking out some of the best products in its long history, more good things should be just around the corner.

▶ *1961 CHEVROLET*

IMPALA SS

Chevrolet inaugurated its celebrated Super Sport nameplate via a $53.80 option package on the 1961 Impala. The SS package's exclusive features included unique "knockoff" hubcaps, thin-stripe whitewall tires, heavy-duty shocks and springs, a steering-column-mounted tach, and bodyside badging. Also debuting this year was the hot new 409 engine, which was rated at 360 horsepower and a whopping 409 pound-feet of torque. It could send an Impala through the quarter mile in 15.8 seconds.

◀ *1962 CHEVROLET*

BEL AIR

The 409 quickly established itself in Super Stock drag racing across the country. Pictured here is Hayden Proffitt wheeling his four-speed 409 Bel Air to Stock Eliminator honors at the 1962 U.S. Nationals. His winning ET was 12.83 seconds at 113.92 mph. Chevrolet now offered a dual four-barrel-carburetor setup on the 409, which helped bump peak horsepower up to 409 and torque up to 420 pound-feet.

▶ *1962 CHEVROLET*

IMPALA SS

Though most drag racers favored the cheaper, lighter Bel Air "bubbletop," the 1962 Impala two-door hardtop cut a sharp figure as well, especially in SS guise. The formal roofline of the hardtop mimicked the look of a top-up convertible. The Impala's flashier trim was highlighted by a brushed-aluminum rear fascia with six taillights instead of the Bel Air's four. Normally, Super Sport Impalas wore full face wheelcovers, but this one sports Bel Air-style "dog-dish" hubcaps for a tougher vibe.

▶ *1962 PONTIAC*
CATALINA

Late in the 1961 model year, Pontiac unleashed its dual-quad Super Duty 421 engine as a purpose-built drag-strip stormer that cranked out at least 405 hp. This '62 Catalina is one of the rare factory lightweight models with aluminum hood, bumper, and front fenders and fender liners. Even the exhaust manifolds on the Super Duty 421 were aluminum, which meant the engine could only be run for short periods of time (like quarter-mile runs). Otherwise, the manifolds were prone to warping from the heat.

◀ *1963 CHEVROLET*
IMPALA Z-11

Chevrolet got into the specialized lightweight factory race-car game with a limited run of just 57 "Z-11" Impalas. All carried a stroked 427-cid version of the 409 with dual-quad carburetors and a very conservative factory rating of 430 hp at 6000 rpm and 425 pound-feet of torque at 4200. Extensive weight-cutting measures included the deletion of the radio, heater, and insulation, plus aluminum front fenders and inner fenders, hood, radiator support panel and fan shroud, and bumpers.

▶ *1963 CHEVROLET*
IMPALA

Legendary race-car builder Smokey Yunick fielded a 1963 Impala at Daytona with Sprint Car driver Johnny Rutherford making his NASCAR debut. The Impala packed a "Mystery Motor" 427-cid V-8 that was a precursor to the production Chevrolet big-block engines that would be introduced a couple years later on production Chevys. The "Mystery" moniker was because the engine was developed in secret, and only a handful of GM insiders and racers like Yunick and Junior Johnson had access to them.

CUTLASS 4-4-2

Oldsmobile rolled out a 4-4-2 option package for its new F-85/Cutlass series in 1964. It was somewhat poorly promoted, however, and only 2999 buyers ordered it. In its first season, 4-4-2 stood for four-barrel carb, four-speed manual transmission, and dual exhausts. The 4-4-2's 330-cid V-8 made 310 hp, 20 more than the regular four-barrel, thanks to a higher-lift cam, heavy-duty bearings, and dual snorkel air cleaner. It turned 0-60 times of 7.5 seconds and 15.5-second quarter miles.

1964 PONTIAC

TEMPEST GTO

The 1964 Pontiac Tempest GTO was the first modern mass-production automobile to put big-cube power in a midsize body—the formula that defined the true muscle car. Pontiac circumvented a GM rule prohibiting intermediates from having V-8s over 330 cid by making its 389-cid V-8 part of an option package, a ploy that did not require corporate approval. The name Gran Turismo Omologato was borrowed from the Ferrari 250 GTO. It stands for a production grand touring machine homologated, or sanctioned, to race.

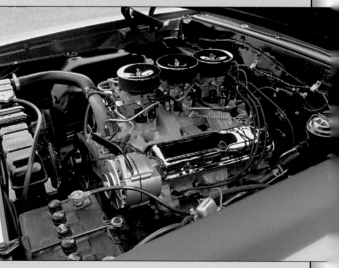

1964 PONTIAC
TEMPEST GTO

GTOs were offered in pillared sport coupe, hardtop coupe, and convertible body styles. The base four-barrel 389 made 325 horsepower, but a desirable Tri-Power three two-barrel carburetor option bumped that figure up to 348 hp. Pontiac hoped to sell a modest 5000 '64 GTOs; final production was 32,450. The GTO was a grand-slam success, and it spurred other manufacturers to create similar machines. The muscle-car era had officially begun.

▶ 1965 BUICK
SKYLARK GS

When GM raised its engine limit for midsize cars to 400 cid, Buick renamed its 401-cid V-8 the "400" and jammed it into the Skylark. The resultant midyear Gran Sport was Buick's first modern muscle car. Its 325 horsepower was less than that of the GTO or 4-4-2, but it had more torque. All Gran Sports got a reinforced convertible frame, dual exhausts, huskier suspension, and bucket seats.

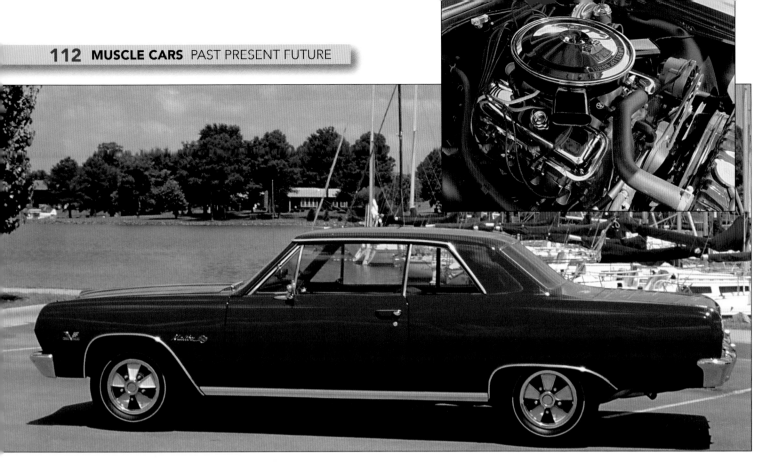

CHEVELLE SS 396 Z-16

Chevy's midsize Chevelle was making the best of its 327-cid V-8s, but it couldn't match the big-block GTO and 4-4-2. That changed at midyear with the Z-16, a 375-hp 396-cid avenger. It was fitted to just 201 Malibu SS models, which got special trim, heavy-duty suspension, and a 160-mph speedometer. It added a substantial $1501.05 to the $2647 base Malibu SS hardtop. The Z-16 Turbo-Jet 396 was basically a hydraulic-lifter version of the 375-hp 396 offered in the Corvette. The Malibu's had a Holley four-barrel and 11.0:1 compression. A Muncie four-speed was mandatory, with axle ratios of up to 4.56:1 available. Mid-14-second quarters at around 100 mph were no sweat.

▼ 1965 PONTIAC
GTO

Technically, the GTO was still a $296 option on the Tempest. The cool-looking hood scoop was nonfunctional, but Pontiac released an over-the-counter option kit for Tri-Power engines that opened the hood scoop and created the Goat's first ram-air setup. Other new options included an $86 Rally cluster with full instrumentation, a $137 AM/FM radio, aluminum front brake drums, and the stamped-steel Rally wheels with functional cooling holes seen on this convertible. GTO ragtop output hit 11,311, and total GTO production soared to 75,352.

▲ 1965 PONTIAC
GTO

While other manufacturers were still hustling to get true muscle cars to market, the GTO (by now affectionately nicknamed the "Goat") had already become a bona-fide pop-culture phenomenon. A handsome body restyle for 1965 was highlighted by stacked headlamps. The 389 V-8 was carried over, but the base version gained 10 horsepower, to 335, and the Tri-Power added 12, to 360, thanks to a revised induction system and improved camshaft profile. A three-speed manual was standard and close- or wide-ratio four-speeds were optional; all had Hurst shifters. A two-speed automatic was also offered.

▲ 1966 BUICK
SKYLARK GRAN SPORT

Fresh sheetmetal gave Buick's Skylark Gran Sport a new look. A new roofline with sail-panel rear pillars was shared by all of GM's 1966 intermediates. Despite the midyear addition of a hotter 340-horsepower version of the 401-cid "Wildcat 445" four-barrel, the Gran Sport was oriented more toward civilized performance, not bare-knuckle street fighting. *Car and Driver's* 340-hp GS with the 3.36:1 axle went to 60 mph in 6.8 seconds, and turned a 14.92 quarter mile at 95 mph. *Motor Trend* managed 7.6 seconds to 60 and 15.47 at 90.54 mph at the strip. Buick built 106,217 Skylarks for 1966; just 13,816 of them were Gran Sports.

▼ 1966 OLDSMOBILE
4-4-2

New sheetmetal and a slightly wider track distinguished the '66 Olds 4-4-2. Still an option, the 4-4-2 package added only $185 to the price of an F-85, $151 to a Cutlass. 4-4-2s gained their own grille and taillamps and a fake front-fender scoop this year. A trifling compression hike brought five extra horses to the standard 400-cid V-8, for a total of 350. For another $110, buyers could get Oldsmobile's first factory tri-carb setup since the late 1950s. It boosted output to 360 hp and cut ETs to the high 14s at 97 mph. Olds also began offering a W-30 cold-air induction system, which included scoops in the front-bumper openings and internal engine mods.

▼ 1966 CHEVROLET
CHEVELLE SS 396

All Chevelle Malibu Super Sports got the 396-cid V-8 for '66, thus earning the SS 396 designation. The base Turbo Jet had 325 hp with a Holley four-barrel. The 360-hp L34 upgrade used a four-bolt-main block and bigger four-barrel. Both had 10.25:1 compression. About 100 cars had a solid-lifter L78, basically an upgrade of the '65 Z-16. It had 375 hp, 11.0:1 compression, and an 800-cfm Holley. A three-speed was standard; four-speed and Powerglide were available. Super Sport styling touches included a blacked-out grille and faux "power bulge" hood scoops. Five-spoke wheelcovers mimicked the look of popular aftermarket "mag" wheels.

▲ 1966 PONTIAC
GTO

Recognizing the GTO's growing popularity, Pontiac promoted it from a Tempest option to a model of its own for 1966. The "Goat" rewarded Pontiac with sales of more than 96,946 units, the highest one-year total ever attained by a true muscle car. And while all GM midsize cars were restyled for '66, none matched the beauty of the GTO's new Coke-bottle contours. This Marina Blue convertible wears the rare red plastic fender liner option. Tri-Power continued as a $113 option, but this would be its last season—at midyear, GM banned all multi-carb packages.

▶ *1966 PONTIAC*

GTO

The GTO was at the height of its popularity, thanks in no small part to Pontiac's canny, "with it" marketing that was perfectly in step with the times. For the 1965 and '66 model years, Pontiac strongly pushed a "Tiger" theme when promoting the GTO. This included live tigers on TV commercials, stuffed tiger tails, and spokesmodels wearing full tiger-print costumes, as seen in this period auto show photograph.

◀ *1967 BUICK*

GS 400

Buick renamed its Gran Sport the GS 400 to denote its new 400-cid V-8, which replaced the old "nailhead" 401-cid design. Like its predecessor, the new 400 had 10.25:1 compression, hydraulic lifters, and made the same 340 horsepower as the top 401. "Your father never told you there'd be Buicks like this," said the ads. Hood scoops on the GS 400 now faced forward, but still weren't functional. The GS 400 helped shake up Buick's staid image, but never had the following of the Chevelle SS 396 or GTO. Sales stayed at around 14,000 for the model year.

1967 CHEVROLET

CAMARO Z/28

Chevrolet answered Ford's Mustang with a dazzling ponycar of its own, the new-for-'67 Camaro. Naturally, high-performance versions were ready almost out of the gate; perhaps the most important was the Z/28. Engineered so Chevrolet could do battle in the SCCA's Trans Am racing series, the Z/28 packed a very potent 302-cid small block, racing stripes, and other upgrades. Just 602 were built.

▲ *1967 CHEVROLET*
CAMARO SS 396

Super Sport Camaros were available right from the start, and SS 396s followed a few months into the model year. The SS 396 initially came in 325-hp tune and tacked $263 on to the SS group. Still later in the year, the 375-hp L78 variant was offered for $500. Stiffened suspension, F70×14 tires, dummy hood vents, woodgrain steering wheel, and bumblebee nose stripe were part of the SS package. First-year Camaro sales trailed Mustang by a wide margin, but of the 220,917 sold, more than 34,000 were Super Sports. Chevy's ponycar was off and running.

▼ *1967 CHEVROLET*
CHEVELLE SS 396

The mildly facelifted Chevelle SS 396 kept the prior year's nonfunctional hood blisters. Underhood changes were also modest. A 325-hp version of the 396 was again standard, while the $105 L34 upgrade went from 360 hp to 350, because of GM's new edict against any car other than Corvette having more than one horsepower per 10 pounds of car weight. At $2825 for the coupe and $3033 for the ragtop, the Super Sports cost about $285 more than comparable Malibu models. A heavy-duty suspension and F70×14 red- or white-stripe tires were part of the package. "If you have a taste for action, here's the satisfier," Chevy said of the SS 396.

▼ *1967 CHEVROLET*
YENKO CAMARO

As the muscle-car craze reached its zenith, many new-car dealerships doubled as speed shops, and a few even produced their own special edition cars. One of the most legendary and successful high-performance dealers was Yenko Chevrolet in Canonsburg, Pennsylvania. Proprietor Don Yenko was quick to realize the Camaro's potential, and produced a limited run of Camaros fitted with the 425-hp Corvette L72 427 V-8. This example wears a fiberglass hood, '67 Corvette side exhaust pipes, and the optional Rally Sport package, which included a slick hidden-headlight grille.

▲ *1967 CHEVROLET*
IMPALA

Chevrolet's full-size cars got a voluptuous new "Coke-bottle" shape for 1967. Even base Impalas could be ordered with the potent 385-hp 427; the Granada Gold Sport Coupe pictured here is so equipped. Aside from the redline tires and the discreet 427 badges on the front fenders, this car is a textbook "sleeper." Mainstream muscle cars were adding more and more "sizzle" in the form of faux scoops, body stripes, and fancy wheel designs, but there also remained serious enthusiasts and street racers who eschewed the extra-cost appearance add-ons. These buyers cared only about maximizing the high-performance bang for their buck, and for them, "stealthy" street machines like this Impala were ideal.

▼ *1967 CHEVROLET*

IMPALA SS 427

By 1967, full-size hot cars had clearly been supplanted by their midsize little brothers, but that didn't stop manufacturers from experimenting with plus-size performance packages. "For the man who'd buy a sports car if it had this much room," was the way Chevrolet promoted the new Impala SS 427. The package included the same 385-hp 427 available on any full-size '67 Chevy, but added stiffer springs and shocks, a front stabilizer bar, and redline tires. Exclusive exterior styling features included a unique domed hood with faux air-intake scoops, blacked-out vertical grille bars, and special emblems. Interestingly, there were no "Impala" badges anywhere on the car. Just 2124 Impala SS 427s were produced this year.

▲ *1967 PONTIAC*

GTO

GTOs saw some visual updates for '67, including a "chain-link" grille and a resculpted tail. The standard engine was now a 400-cid enlargement of the 389-cid V-8. Compression was unchanged, and the base four-barrel engine again made 335 hp. But taking over the 360-hp slot from the discontinued tri-carb setup was a new four-barrel High Output option. It cost $77 extra and included a higher-lift cam, free-flow exhaust manifolds, and an open-element air cleaner.

▲ *1967 PONTIAC*

FIREBIRD 400

Pontiac rolled out its own ponycar just a few months after the Camaro appeared. The Firebird wore Pontiac's signature styling cues well, especially the "beaked" nose and split-grille treatment. The brawniest Firebirds were the Firebird 400 models, which packed a 325-hp 400-cid V-8. Hood scoops wearing "400" badges were part of the package. In the background of this shot is General Motors' first Firebird, the outlandish XP-21 Firebird I dream car of 1954.

▼ *1968 BUICK*

GS 400

All GM intermediates got a groundbreaking redesign for 1968, with fuselage-like contours and rooflines that flowed smoothly into the rear fenders. However, with its semi-skirted rear wheel openings and breezy bodyside character line, the Buick Skylark lost a lot of its macho attitude in the process. GS 400s still had a 340-hp 400, however, and a new dealer-installed "Stage 1 Special Package" added a hotter cam, stronger valve springs, and other hop-ups for an under-rated 345 horsepower.

▲ *1968 CHEVROLET*
CAMARO Z/28

The $400 Z/28 package entered its sophomore year with few changes, though it now had fender emblems. Its 302-cid engine was created by putting the crankshaft from a 283 V-8 into a 327 block to get under the SCCA's 305-cid limit for its Trans Am road-racing series. The big bore and short stroke let the engine rev to 7200 rpm, and it was conservatively rated at 290 hp. Detail changes on all '68 Camaros included side-marker lights and the deletion of vent windows.

▼ *1968 CHEVROLET*
CHEVY II NOVA

The redesigned 1968 Chevy II Novas wore a scaled-down version of the '68 Chevelle's new shape. In short order, the new Novas became fodder for dealer tuners. In 1968, Fred Gibb Chevrolet of LaHarpe, Illinois, ordered 50 specially built SS Novas with the 375-hp 395-cid V-8 and Turbo 400 automatic. Some of these cars were modified into "Super-Chevy IIs" by noted drag racer Dick Harrell. They came complete with Harrell-prepared 450-hp, 427-cid V-8s. Harrell's Performance Center also added a fiberglass hood and Cragar S/S wheels.

▲ *1968 CHEVROLET*
YENKO CAMARO

Yenko Chevrolet was still serving up its own special brand of "Super Camaro." As in 1967, Don Yenko would order SS 396 Camaros from the factory, then swap out the 375-hp L78 396 for a 425-hp L72 427. Heavy-duty suspension, a 4.10:1 Positraction rear end, and a 140-mph speedometer were specially installed at the factory. Yenko badges and a twin-scooped fiberglass hood with tie-down pins were also part of the package. It's estimated that just 65 of these boulevard beasties were built for '68. Most wore Pontiac Rally II wheels with unique "Y" center caps.

▲ *1968 CHEVROLET*
CHEVELLE SS 396

The Malibu/Chevelle was handsomely redesigned for 1968. SS 396s (which were now a distinct series) got a blacked-out grille and rear panel and light-colored cars got a dark lower body treatment. The "double-dome" hood theme was carried over and F70×14 tires were made standard. Front disc brakes were a $100 option. The base 396 again had 325 hp, but another $237 netted the 375-hp L78, which had solid lifters, big-port heads, and an 800-cfm Holley four-barrel on a low-rise aluminum manifold. Just 4751 SS 396s were ordered with the L78.

▼ 1968 OLDSMOBILE
4-4-2

A curvaceous 1968 redesign for midsize Oldsmobiles agreed with the 4-4-2's classy-yet-brawny image. The base powerplant continued to be the 400-cubic-inch Rocket with 10.5:1 compression and a four-barrel carburetor. Manually shifted cars received a 350-horsepower V-8, while those with Turbo Hydra-matic had to make do with 25 less. The ultimate 4-4-2 carried a potent W-30 force-air-induced version (with scoops now mounted below the bumper) rated at 360 hp.

▼ 1968 OLDSMOBILE
HURST/OLDS

Hurst modified 451 Cutlass hardtops and 64 pillared coupes with 455-cid V-8s to create the first Hurst/Olds. They had the factory's Force Air system, which used under-bumper air inlets to feed twin air-cleaner snorkels. Cars with air conditioning had 389 hp, others had 390, but all got automatics with Hurst Dual-Gate shifters. Custom silver and black paint and wood dashboard trim were standard. The Hurst/Olds's outstanding power, fuss-free performance, full warranty, and exclusivity came at $1161 over the sticker of a regular 4-4-2.

▲ 1968 OLDSMOBILE
4-4-2

Encouraged by the 4-4-2's reception, Oldsmobile upgraded it to full-series status for 1968. In addition to hardtop and pillared-coupe body styles, a handsome convertible version was also offered. The 4-4-2 buyer continued to get a lot of heavy-duty equipment, including beefier shocks, springs, and sway bars; high-performance tires, and wider wheels. Automatic transmissions became available in a 4-4-2 in 1965, so the name now stood for 400 cid, four-barrel carburetor, and dual exhaust. The 4-4-2 ragtops started at $3341, hardtop coupes at $3150.

▲ 1968 PONTIAC
FIREBIRD 400

Firebird styling was unchanged for 1968, save for the deletion of side vent windows and the addition of federally mandated fender marker lights. Horsepower on the standard 400-cid V-8 increased by five, to 330. Ram Air continued as the rarest and strongest engine option at about $600 more than the regular 400. It again had a hotter cam, stronger valve springs, and exclusive use of functional hood scoops. At midyear, the 335-hp Ram Air mill was replaced by the 340-hp Ram Air II.

◀ *1968 PONTIAC*
FIREBIRD 400

A third Firebird 400 engine variation debuted for 1968, and was the best blend of machismo and manners. The 400 HO, or High Output, cost about $350 over the base 400 and used free-flow exhausts and, when hooked to a four-speed, its own revised cam. It too was rated at 335 hp, but it redlined higher than the base engine and below the Ram Air.

1968 PONTIAC
GTO

GTOs got a dazzling new shape with an energy-absorbing Endura front bumper for 1968. Hidden headlamps were so popular that most people didn't realize they were an option, as were dual exhaust splitters, a hood-mounted tach, and functional Ram Air scoops. Top GTO engine choice was the 366-hp Ram Air II 400. Pontiac president John Z. DeLorean (right) was perhaps at the peak of his career in the late 1960s. He was promoted to run Pontiac in 1965 at age 40, making him the youngest division head in GM history, and a string of home-run new Pontiac introductions followed. The redesigned GTO netted *Motor Trend*'s Car of the Year award for 1968, thanks in part to its trendsetting front end.

▲ 1969 CHEVROLET
CAMARO Z/28

New sheetmetal gave '69 Camaros a huskier look, but engine choices mostly stayed the same. The Z/28 package had fully come into its own by now, and the sales figures proved it. Production nearly tripled, to 20,302. Mechanically, the package saw little change, but a bulged "cowl induction" hood was a new $79 option. It had a valve that snapped open at 80-percent throttle to draw in cool air from the base of the windshield. Four-wheel disc brakes were optional on all Camaros this year, but only 206 got them; the $500 price tag likely discouraged shoppers.

▲ 1969 CHEVROLET
CAMARO RS/SS

The Rally Sport option package carried over to the revamped-for-'69 Camaro body. It now included hidden headlamps with headlamp washers and triple-glass windows for "flash-to-pass" signaling. The vacuum-operated headlamp covers powered aside for nighttime driving. A damage-resistant body-color front bumper was a new Camaro option. This Olympic Gold RS/SS coupe packs the hottest engine available in a regular-production "over-the-counter" 1969 Camaro: a 375-horsepower L78 396-cubic-inch V-8, here hooked to a Muncie M21 four-speed transmission and Positraction 12-bolt rear end with a 3.55:1 gear ratio.

▼ 1969 CHEVROLET
CAMARO ZL1

This unassuming LeMans Blue coupe is one of the rarest and most exotic Camaros ever built. It's one of just 69 equipped with the awesome ZL1 V-8—an aluminum-head, aluminum-block 427. The ZL1 was factory rated at 430 horsepower, but actual output was more than 500. And it weighed just 500 pounds—about the same as Chevy's 327-cid V-8. The production ZL1 Camaros were built primarily to qualify the engine for NHRA racing, and were sparsely equipped—though the engine alone added a staggering $4160 to the cost of the car, pushing the total sticker price to a stratospheric $7200. The ZL1 engine also went into two production Corvettes.

▼ 1969 CHEVROLET
YENKO/SC CAMARO

By 1969, Don Yenko had found a better way to produce his 427 Super Camaros. Instead of his dealership performing laborious Camaro engine swaps on its own, Yenko began utilizing Chevrolet's Central Office Production Order procedure. The "COPO" system was intended to satisfy special requests from nonperformance fleet buyers, but Yenko was able to bend the rules and use it to order a limited run of Camaros with the L72 427 (which Yenko rated at 450 hp) and other special equipment installed at the factory. His dealership would then apply Yenko stripes and badging (including "SYC" headrest logos) and other speed equipment if the buyer desired.

▲ 1969 CHEVROLET
NOVA SS 396

When the Chevy II Novas were redesigned for 1968, they shared their chassis design with the Camaro, so big-block engines finally fit. Chevrolet abandoned the "Chevy II" moniker for 1969, but Novas were little changed otherwise. As with the Camaro, the hottest regular-production Nova engine was the 375-hp L78 396. Visual cues to the SS Novas included simulated air intakes on the hood, blacked-out front grille and taillight panel, and specific badging.

▲ 1969 CHEVROLET
CHEVELLE SS 396

The Chevelle SS 396 became a $348 Malibu option for 1969, but that didn't dim sales, which hit a record 86,307. The 375-horsepower L78 396 V-8 was again the top engine option. An estimated 400 buyers shelled out an additional $395 for the L89 option, which fit the L78 with weight-saving aluminum heads. A very mild facelift for '69 gave all Chevelles an attractive new grille and larger taillights, but the SS 396's "power bulge" hood was still just for show.

▼ 1969 CHEVROLET
YENKO/SC NOVA

Dropping the fire-breathing L72 427 V-8 into Chevy's compact made for an especially wild Nova that even Don Yenko himself feared. It had the same hyper-performance powertrain as Yenko's COPO Camaros and Chevelles, but less mass and better weight distribution than either. And it was even faster. Just 37 were built. The Yenko/SC (for "Super Car") 427 Novas were not COPO cars; they were factory-built 396 Novas that received the 427 transplant at the Yenko dealership.

▼ 1969 CHEVROLET
YENKO/SC CHEVELLE

By using Chevrolet's COPO system, Yenko Chevrolet and a handful of other high-performance dealers were able to circumvent GM's ban of engines over 400 cubic inches in midsize cars. All COPO Chevelles had front disc brakes and a 12-bolt Positraction rear axle with 4.10:1 gears, and were available with either a Muncie four-speed or the Turbo 400 Hydra-matic. Just 323 COPO 427 Chevelles were produced for 1969 and, of those, only 99 became Yenko/SCs.

▼ 1969 CHEVROLET

IMPALA

Full-size Chevys got new bodywork for 1969 that included rectangular taillights and a wrap-around front bumper/grille arrangement. Base Impala Sport Coupes such as this one wore a less formal roofline than their pricier Impala Custom siblings. The Impala SS was still around for its swan-song season in 1969, packing a 427 as standard equipment. However, any Impala could be equipped with 427 power. The unusually-optioned example shown here is one of just 546 ordered with the 425-hp L72 427. It also packs a Muncie four-speed.

▲ 1969 OLDSMOBILE

4-4-2 W-30

Oldsmobile's 4-4-2 was back with few changes for 1969. Its 400-cid V-8 had 350 hp with manual transmission and 325 with automatic. The blueprinted W-30 version returned, while the new W-32 package combined the 350-hp variant with automatic transmission. The Force Air option again earned a 360-hp rating with the four-speed. Olds launched its wacky "Dr. Oldsmobile" ad campaign this year, which featured a fictitious mad scientist with a silent-movie moustache and baggy lab coat concocting potent "W-Machines" with the help of some ghoulish sidekicks.

1969 OLDSMOBILE

4-4-2

Oldsmobile produced 4296 4-4-2 convertibles for 1969. Just 121 of those had the W-30 upgrade and only 91 of those had the four-speed transmission. This correctly restored Saffron Yellow ragtop is probably the best example known to have survived. The original sticker price of $4203.69 included such options as power steering ($100.05), deluxe pushbutton radio ($69.51), Super Stock II wheels ($73.72), sports console ($61.09), tinted glass ($38.97), close-ratio four-speed manual transmission ($184.80), and, of course, the W-30 package ($263.30).

▶ *1969 OLDSMOBILE*
HURST/OLDS PROTOTYPE

The Hurst/Olds returned for 1969, but no longer was it remotely low-key in silver and black. Bold "Firemist Gold" striping now accented its white paint. On the hood was a flamboyant dual-snout scoop more efficient at feeding the engine than the under-bumper inlets on other 4-4-2s. And the decklid held an enormous air foil that furnished 15 pounds of downforce at 60 mph, 64 pounds at 120 mph. This photo shows not the production car, but a prototype that was photographed on December 6, 1968, at GM's Tech Center. The striping design was more or less dialed in at this point, but the hood scoop, rear air foil, and bodyside badges were still unsettled. The Cragar S/S wheels shown here wouldn't make it to the production car either.

▼ *1969 PONTIAC*
FIREBIRD TRANS AM

It debuted midway through the 1969 model year as an unsung option package, but Trans Am would become one of Pontiac's most significant performance cars. To the Firebird it added a functional twin-scoop hood, rear spoiler, open fender vents, and a unique white and blue paint scheme. Standard was the 335-hp Ram Air 400. A 345-hp Ram Air IV upgrade was optional. Bucket seats, console, and specially tuned steering and suspension were included on all T/As.

▲ *1969 PONTIAC*
FIREBIRD 400

Like their Chevy Camaro cousins, Pontiac Firebirds got new sheetmetal for 1969 that was highlighted by an Endura plastic front end with a smaller split grille. Firebird 400 remained the muscular version, with its 330-hp 400-cid V-8. Also included were twin hood scoops, special handling suspension, and chrome engine dress-up components. The top engine option was the 345-horse Ram Air IV 400. Total Firebird sales slumped to 75,362 coupes and 11,649 ragtops.

◀ *1969 PONTIAC*

GTO

"The Great One" got minor styling updates for 1969 that included an eggcrate-style grille, revised front parking lamps, and a new rear bumper. Vent windows were deleted. The "Goat" two-door hardtop accounted for 64,851 sales, second in popularity only to the LeMans hardtop coupe. Hood-mounted tachometers like the one seen on this GTO were an extra-cost option that was something of a Pontiac staple. They looked cool but were often hard to read at night or in bright, glaring sunlight.

▶ *1969 PONTIAC*

GTO JUDGE

The GTO lineup got a whimsical new performance model for 1969. Pontiac added op-art decals, a rear spoiler, and a 366-hp Ram Air III 400 to create The Judge, a $332 option package on the GTO. The car's name was a sly pop-culture reference—"Here come da Judge" was a recurring catchphrase on the popular TV show *Laugh-In*. The first 5000 Judges were painted Carousel Red (a bright shade of orange) but other colors were offered. The 370-hp Ram Air IV was a $390 Judge option.

▶ *1969 PONTIAC*

ROYAL BOBCAT GTO

The most famous Pontiac performance retailer of the Sixties was Ace Wilson's Royal Pontiac in Royal Oak, Michigan. The dealership fielded several Pontiac drag cars and offered hopped-up "Royal Bobcat" Pontiacs throughout the decade. This GTO is a one-of-a-kind factory test car that was fitted with an experimental 400-cid Ram Air V engine that put out about 500 horsepower, but never actually saw production.

▶ *1970 BUICK*
GS STAGE 1

Buick's restyled Skylark again hosted the GS models, which started with a 325 hp 350 V-8. Replacing the 400-cid V-8 was a big-valve, hot cam 455 with 350 horsepower. The new top dog was the $199 Stage 1 performance package for the 455. It added a higher-lift cam, even-larger valves, and tighter compression for 360 hp with the same earth-moving 510 pound-feet of torque as the regular 455. A 3.64:1 Positraction axle was included with either the four-speed or the automatic.

1970 BUICK
GSX

The 1970 GSX with optional 455-cube Stage 1 mill was the ultimate expression of Buick's ultimate supercar. The package added an upgraded suspension, hood tach, stripes, spoilers, and $1195 to a GS 455. Eye-grabbing Saturn Yellow or Apollo White were the only available colors. Of the 687 GSXs built, 488 were ordered with the Stage 1 upgrade, which cost $113 on a GSX. The fact that even GM's reserved, upscale Buick division saw fit to release a vehicle as outlandish as the GSX is evidence of how thoroughly the muscle-car craze had taken hold by 1970.

▶ *1970 CHEVROLET*

CAMARO Z28

After a production delay, the all-new 1970 Camaros finally hit the streets in February 1970. This classic redesign was the foundation for the finest Z28 of the muscle era. Hood and decklid stripes, black grille, and seven-inch-wide mag-type steel wheels were part of the package; the cowl-induction hood was dropped. A short rear decklid spoiler was standard, but this example wears an optional larger version, as well as the optional front spoiler. The new Z28 engine was Corvette's exhilarating solid-lifter 350-cubic-inch "LT1" four-barrel, here rated at 360 horsepower. Suspension advances made all '70 Camaros good handlers, and the Z28, with its firmer underpinnings and sticky Polyglas F60×15 tires, was a world-class road car.

▼ *1970 CHEVROLET*

CHEVELLE SS 396

Sheetmetal changes freshened Chevelle and the $445 SS package again came with a 396, but it was now the 350-hp L34 version. In January 1970, a 350-hp, 402-cid V-8 replaced it, but the "396" label stuck. SSs got a beefed suspension with a rear stabilizer bar, plus seven-inch sport wheels on F70×14 white-letter tires. A new option was the $147 domed hood. It featured a vacuum-operated cowl-induction flap that opened under full throttle. The new Chevelle looked plenty tough, but the competition was tough too, and SS 396 production fell to 53,559.

▲ *1970 CHEVROLET*

CAMARO SS/RS

SS models rounded out Camaro's performance lineup for 1970. The SS 350 featured a tamer 300-hp 350, but the rarely seen SS 396 was offered in 350- and, by special order, 375-hp versions of Chevy's big-block V-8, which by this point actually displaced 402 cubic inches. This SS Camaro is equipped with the $168.55 Rally Sport option package, which included a distinctive split-bumper nose with a soft Endura grille surround and round parking lamps. Camaro convertibles were discontinued this year, leaving the coupe as the lone Camaro body style.

1970 CHEVROLET
CHEVELLE SS 454 LS6

When GM lifted its displacement ban on midsize cars, Chevy responded with a monster 454-cubic-inch V-8 that *started* at 360 horsepower and topped out at an attention-getting 450—the highest factory horsepower rating of the original muscle-car era. This ultimate 454 was called LS6, and came with an 800-cfm Holley four-barrel on an aluminum intake, 11.25:1 compression, solid lifters, and four-bolt mains. Performance, naturally, was awesome: *Hot Rod's* LS6 SS 454 clipped off a 13.4-second quarter mile at 108.7 mph. Altogether, Chevy built 8773 SS 454s for '70, split about evenly between the LS6 and the more manageable LS5.

▶ 1970 OLDSMOBILE
CUTLASS W-31

Kooky Dr. Oldsmobile and his odd minions were still hamming it up in 1970 Oldsmobile performance-car advertising. The prices of many high-end muscle cars were out of reach for many young enthusiasts, so manufacturers began offering more-affordable options that offered most of the "show," but not quite as much "go." The Oldsmobile Cutlass W-31 package brought many of the appearance and handling goodies of the 4-4-2, but packed a 325-horsepower 350 small-block in place of the 4-4-2's thumping 455.

▼ *1970 OLDSMOBILE*

RALLYE 350

What the Olds Rallye 350 lacked in outright muscle, it made up for in ostentatiousness. This budget-friendly junior muscle car stood out from the pack via Sebring Yellow body paint (the only color available), urethane-coated body-color bumpers, blackout grille, and black/orange accent striping with Rallye 350 insignia. A rear airfoil could be added for another $74. The sole engine was a 310-hp 350 that utilized the 4-4-2's fiberglass cold-air-induction hood.

▼ *1970 PONTIAC*

FIREBIRD FORMULA 400

Just like their Camaro cousins, Pontiac Firebirds received a radical, groundbreaking redesign for 1970. The new Firebird's sophisticated, European-inspired body shape was cutting-edge, as was its color-keyed Endura plastic nose. The entry-level performance versions were now dubbed Formula 400, and wore an aggressive-looking twin-scooped fiberglass hood. Included in the Formula 400's base price of $3370 was a 330-horsepower four-barrel 400 V-8.

▲ *1970 OLDSMOBILE*

4-4-2 W-30

For 1970, Oldsmobile introduced perhaps the best all-around 4-4-2 ever. The major advance was the newly standard 455-cubic-inch big-block V-8, an under-stressed, big-port engine with tugboat torque. It made 365 hp in base form, an underrated 370 in W-30 guise. A stylish facelift brought a fresh front bumper and a rear-bumper/taillight design. The W-30 package included a fiberglass hood with functional scoops, plastic inner fenders, and less sound deadening than other 4-4-2s. The rear-deck spoiler could be deleted. Hardtop 4-4-2s started at $3376.

▲ *1970 PONTIAC*

TRANS AM

With the introduction of the second-generation Firebird, Pontiac's Trans Am came into its own as a bare-knuckles brawler. Functional spoilers and vents abounded, while super-tough underpinnings and quickened steering gave it corner-hungry handling. The standard Trans Am engine was a Ram Air 400 rated at 345 horsepower; the optional Ram Air IV 400 had 370. The shaker scoop mounted directly to the motor; Pontiac said it drew in cool air from the windshield base. The Endura nosepiece sported the first of the T/A's "screaming chicken" decals.

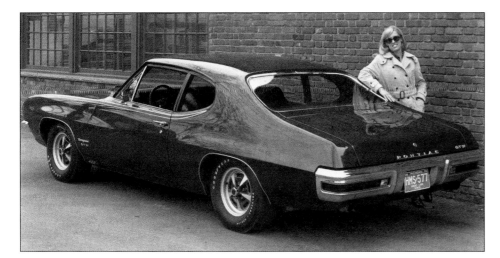

▲ 1970 PONTIAC
TEMPEST GT-37

The styling of all midsize Pontiacs was significantly updated for 1970. The Tempest, LeMans, and LeMans Sport received a new bumper/grille design that bore a passing resemblance to the 1969 Firebird. Sculpted bodysides featured attractive new character lines that flared out above the wheels, and the rear bumper was redesigned to house wraparound taillights. Pontiac issued a "budget performance" GT-37 package at midseason that added a Hurst-shifted three-speed, hood-lock pins, Rally II wheels on F70×14 white-letter tires, dual exhaust with rear-valance tips, GT-37 badges, and '69 Judge-style stripes to V-8 Tempest coupes and hardtop coupes.

▲ 1970 PONTIAC
GTO

The GTO's optional 455 engine made just 10 more horsepower than the standard 350-hp 400, but its 500 pound-feet of torque added considerable grunt. Hobbled by a strike that cost 67 days of production, plus rising inflation and insurance costs that were squeezing prospective customers, the GTO saw its production fall off substantially in 1970. The total came to 40,149—the fewest since the nameplate's debut in 1964—of which 36,366 were hardtop coupes. This one wears the optional but seldom-seen 1969 Judge-style bodyside sport stripes.

▼ 1970 PONTIAC
GTO

The 1970 GTOs received an new all-Endura nose with twin grille openings; disappearing headlamps were no longer offered. The big news was under the hood: a 455-cid V-8 was available and had 360 hp (or 370 when hooked to the standard three-speed manual). It joined the carried-over 400, which made 350 hp in standard tune, 366 with Ram Air III, and 370 with Ram Air IV. This GTO convertible wears redline tires, but they were fast becoming passé by 1970; most muscle cars had switched to raised-white-letter tires as factory equipment. The GTO's popularity was starting to slip a bit this year; convertible production hit only 3783 cars.

▼ 1970 PONTIAC
GTO JUDGE

As the GTO evolved into a luxury-muscle intermediate, the Judge clung to its adolescent roots. Few cars made a bolder visual statement. "The Judge" decals returned, multi-hued stripes appeared over the bodyside creases, and the 60-inch rear wing now stood high and proud on the tail. Orbit Orange was a 1970-only color exclusive to Judges, and was teamed with combination blue/orange/pink stripes. The Judge gained the Ram Air III 400 as standard, with Ram Air IV optional. It could get the 455-cubic-inch V-8 late in the model year. The Judge package was a $337 option for 1970, and of 3797 built, just 168 were ragtops.

▲ 1971 BUICK
GS 455

The Stage 1 package was ordered on only 801 GS coupes and 81 ragtops for 1971, a sign of the muscle car's waning popularity with the new-car-buying public. There was just one GS series now; a 260-hp small-block 350 was standard, and a 315-hp 455 was optional. Power was down to 345 hp in top-line Stage 1 form. All 1971 GS engines were detuned to run on low-lead fuel. *Motor Trend*'s 1971 Stage 1 did the quarter in 14.7 seconds at 92.5 mph. That was three-quarters of a second longer and eight mph slower than the 1970 GSX, as reported by *Road Test*.

▼ 1971 CHEVROLET
CAMARO Z28

Partly because of the short 1970 model run, changes for 1971 Camaros were minor: High-back bucket seats, plus a cushioned-center steering wheel on Sport Coupe and RS models and a new sport steering wheel for the SS and Z28. Engines were detuned to run on regular gas, and horsepower ratings were reported in more-realistic net figures instead of gross numbers. The Z28, now rated at 275 horsepower net and with lowered compression, watched output plummet from 8733 units in 1970 to 4862 for 1971. A good Z28 could turn a 14.9 quarter.

▼ 1971 BUICK
GSX

The GSX was downgraded to an option package instead of a stand-alone model for 1971, but available colors were expanded from two to six. The package included bodyside stripes, hood paint, GSX emblems, and rear spoiler. The GSX's front spoiler, body-color rear spoiler, hood tachometer, and sport mirrors were now available as individual options on any GS model. All Skylarks got minor styling tweaks that included new front and rear bumpers and a revised grille texture. The GSX survived—barely—into 1972; the option was dropped after a run of just 44 cars.

▼ 1971 CHEVROLET
CHEVELLE HEAVY CHEVY

Chevrolet added a "Heavy Chevy" option package midway through the 1971 model year for base Chevelle coupes. Conceived as a way to sidestep the hefty insurance surcharges on SS Chevelles, the Heavy Chevy option package delivered muscle-car "sizzle" without as much "steak." Included were a blackout grille, domed hood with hood-lock pins, 14×6 rally wheels, and Heavy Chevy decals and bodyside stripes in black or white. Bucket seats weren't available, however. The package could be ordered with any V-8 engine except the 454, which was reserved for SS models.

▶ *1971 CHEVROLET*
CHEVELLE SS

The impact of the fast-changing muscle-car landscape was obvious in the 1971 Chevelle SS line, where small blocks re-emerged in the form of two 350-cid V-8s: a 245-hp two-barrel and a 270-hp four-barrel. But big-block power was still available. The 402 four-barrel cost $173 and had 300 horsepower, 50 below the previous year's base SS engine. To retain the hallowed SS 396 badging, Chevy had called the 1970 402 a "396." For '71, it was renamed the "Turbo Jet 400."

▲ *1971 CHEVROLET*
CHEVELLE SS 454

The basic SS package offered a lot for its $357 asking price: the F41 suspension with front and rear stabilizer bars, power front discs, wider F60 tires on larger 15-inch five-spoke wheels, and blackout grille. All Chevelles got single headlamps borrowed from the Monte Carlo and a new rear bumper with round taillights. The SS could be spiffed up with optional racing stripes and the extra-cost Cowl Induction hood. The top engine choice was the hydraulic-lifter LS5 454-cubic-inch V-8, which made 365 horsepower and added $279 to the cost of an SS Chevelle. Interestingly, only LS5 cars carried external engine ID; their badges said "454." All others wore simple "SS" insignia. That was a pretty revealing sign of the times. For 1971, Chevy built 19,293 Chevelle SSs (including El Caminos); 9502 had the 454 V-8.

▼ *1971 OLDSMOBILE*
4-4-2 W-30

Olds followed GM's lead and detuned its engines for 1971, but the 4-4-2 W-30 package still meant a factory-blueprinted 455-cid V-8 with air-induction hood. However, under GM's net horsepower system (measuring output with all accessories in place), the base 455 got a rating of 260 horsepower and the W-30 a rating of 300 hp. The 4-4-2 now came only as a $3552 coupe weighing 3688 pounds or a $3743 convertible at 3731 pounds. The W-30 package added $369. The W-32 and 350-cubic-inch W-31 packages were dropped for '71.

▶ *1971 PONTIAC*
FIREBIRD FORMULA

Firebird changed little after its short 1970 model year, though Formula 350 and 455 models joined the Formula 400. All engines followed GM's new corporate edict to run on unleaded fuel, in anticipation of the new federal emissions standards that were just around the corner. Louvered vents behind the front wheels were a new touch on all Firebirds except Trans Am. T/As may have had the "look-at-me" scoops, spoilers, and paint, but the clean, unadorned shape of the Firebird Formula made a strong statement as well.

▲ *1971 PONTIAC*
TRANS AM

The Trans Am was unchanged externally, but packed a strong new 335-horsepower 455 HO engine underhood. This mill was also offered in the cheaper Formula, however, and sales of the $4590 T/A fell to just 2116. Still, the fast-changing muscle-car landscape meant that GTO sales were falling off fast too. Despite coming close to cancellation itself, it turned out the Trans Am would take over the role of Pontiac's premier performance car from the fast-fading GTO, and outlive it as well.

▼ *1971 PONTIAC*
GT-37

Come 1971, Pontiac's entry-level midsize-car lineup lost its Tempest nameplate in favor of the more-obscure T-37 moniker. The GT-37 package was again intended to attract performance-minded but cash-strapped buyers. It was available with the two-barrel 350 V-8, the four-barrel 400, and the four-barrel 455, and consisted of the same basic dress-up equipment as in 1970 with the addition of some new bodyside stripes. Pontiac's 1971 catalog claimed, "There's a little GTO in every GT-37, and you don't have to be over 30 to afford it!" The GT-37 never caught on with buyers, however, and the package was dropped after a minuscule 1971 production run.

▲ 1971 PONTIAC
GTO JUDGE

GTOs got a new hood and revised front fascia for 1971. Judges came standard with the top GTO engine available, the 335-hp 455 HO (for High Output). The Judge ran the quarter in 14.9 for *Motor Trend*, compared to a 15.4 at 92 mph for a 300-hp 400-cid GTO. Zero-60 times were 7.0 for the Judge, 7.1 for the Goat. Both test cars were equipped with a four-speed and a 3.55:1 rear axle. Insurance rates and changing tastes caused total GTO production to dwindle to 10,532, and the Judge was retired in mid-1971 after just 374 had been built.

▲ 1972 BUICK
GS

The flashy GSX was discontinued, and Buick built just 8575 GS models for 1972—even after dropping prices $60-$70 to spur sales. The base price of a GS hardtop was $3225. The convertible started at $3406, and just 852 examples were built. A large sliding fabric sunroof was a novel option this year. The Stage 1 455 remained available, but it was down to 270 horsepower. Despite the lower rated power, a 1972 Stage 1 GS was still quick; *Motor Trend* clocked 0-60 mph in 5.8 seconds and 14.1 at 97 mph for the quarter mile.

▼ 1971 PONTIAC
GTO JUDGE

Pontiac's potent Ram Air engines were discontinued this year as GM lowered compression ratios to allow the use of unleaded fuel. The '71 455 HO had fewer horses than the previous optional Ram Air IV 400, but it had much more torque at lower rpm. Not exactly tractable, it was still better behaved on the street than the high-strung 400 IV. This Tropic Green ragtop is one of only 17 Judge convertibles built. Optional "honeycomb" wheels offered a distinctive appearance on Pontiac performance cars this year, but were especially heavy due to their polyurethane/steel construction.

▲ 1972 CHEVROLET
CHEVELLE SS

This was the last year for true Chevelle Super Sport muscle. The top power option, the 454 LS5, was down to 270 net horsepower; the Turbo-Jet "400" fell to 240. The LS5 went into just 5333 cars, mostly hardtops. Base SS power was a 130-hp 307, and docile 165- and 175-horse small blocks were optional. Another sign of worsening muscle-car times: The "performance" axle was a 3.31:1. Among other minor detail changes, Chevelle lost its prominent central grille bar this year, but styling was mostly a 1971 repeat. The Super Sport package itself was also little changed. Total SS production fell to 24,946.

▶ *1972 OLDSMOBILE*

4-4-2 W-30

Oldsmobile demoted the 4-4-2 to an appearance and handling option on select Cutlass models for 1972. The package included the expected stripe decals and badging, plus the FE2 suspension with heavy-duty front and rear stabilizer bars, Hurst competition shifter, 14×7-inch wheels, louvered hood, and special 4-4-2 grille. All manufacturers now reported net horsepower and torque figures instead of gross ratings. The 4-4-2's standard engine was now a 160-hp 350-cube two-barrel V-8, with a 180-hp four-barrel version optional. The next step up was a four-barrel 455, which made 250 horsepower with the Turbo 400 automatic transmission and 270 with the M20 four-speed. The top power option was still the W-30: a factory-blueprinted four-barrel 455 with 300 hp. Priced at a healthy $599, it again included a twin-scooped fiberglass Cold-Air induction hood. Performance was still respectable: *Motor Trend*'s 4-4-2 W-30 did the 0-60 sprint in 6.6 seconds and the quarter mile in 14.5.

◀ *1972 OLDSMOBILE*

4-4-2 W-30

The last 4-4-2 convertibles were built this year, as the body style would not survive to 1973. Total 4-4-2 production actually rose a bit over 1971, ending at 9845 units. Of those, just 772 were W-30s. After testing the 1972 4-4-2, *Motor Trend* said, "...last year's compression drop was rather like hitting Dr. Oldsmobile with a malpractice suit. But there's still some soul left in Lansing, and despite all the furor, a 4-4-2 will still churn up all the smoke and fury the average muscle car driver could need and probably handle."

▶ *1972 PONTIAC*
FIREBIRD FORMULA

The 1972 Firebirds were visually unchanged save for the deletion of 1971's front-fender vents and a honeycomb mesh grille insert that nicely matched the available honeycomb wheels. The '72 Formula 400 stickered at $3221. Sales continued to nosedive, however, so the entire Firebird line was on thin ice—total 1972 Firebird output plummeted 44 percent, and only 5250 Formula-series Firebirds were sold for 1972.

▼ *1972 PONTIAC*
TRANS AM

Trans Ams continued as racy as ever, and the price was cut $340 to $4256 list, presumably to spark sales. But the public's continued drift away from performance combined with a factory strike to hold T/A production to just 1286 for the model year. Trans Am's shaker-hood 455 returned with 300 net horsepower, down from 1971's 335 gross figure. Torque also fell. A four-speed manual transmission replaced a three-speed as standard. *Car and Driver* ran one with 3.42:1 gears to 60 mph in just 5.4 seconds and through the quarter at 13.9 at 104.6 mph.

▲ *1972 PONTIAC*
GTO

A revised grille texture and front-fender air extractor vents identified 1972 GTOs, which reverted to option-package status. Of the 5807 ordered, all but 134 were hardtops; the rest were pillared coupes. The "ducktail" rear spoiler seen on this example was an extremely rare extra-cost item. Base power came from a 400-cubic-inch V-8 now rated at 250 net horsepower. The "regular" optional 455 also made 250 hp and could be had only with an automatic. The top engine option was a 300-hp 455 HO. *Motor Trend*'s 455 HO four-speed with 3.55:1 gears turned a 15.4 at 92 mph. *MT* said the 455's cam shook the whole car at idle. The engine had a tendency to bog so it had to be launched at 3400 rpm, thereby incurring massive wheelspin.

▶ *1973 CHEVROLET*

CHEVELLE SS

The Super Sport package was carried into 1973 on the new Colonnade Chevelles. Though the SS option hung on for years in El Caminos, this year would mark its final appearance on Chevelles. A black-finished grille, bodyside striping, prominent SS badging, and a Monte Carlo-style instrument panel were all part of the package. Hefty front and rear bumpers were a bit unsightly, but necessary to meet the new federal five-mph impact standards. Super Sport buyers had their choice of three engines: a 145-hp two-barrel 350, a 175-hp four-barrel 350, or a 245-hp four-barrel 454 big block.

▲ *1973 CHEVROLET*

BALDWIN-MOTION PHASE III CHEVELLE

A handful of independent dealers still dared to offer unfettered muscle machines even as the federal hammer came down on the Detroit automakers, but their days were numbered too. Muscle-car tuner Joel Rosen's Motion Performance and Baldwin Chevrolet, both in Long Island, New York, had been offering no-holds-barred Baldwin-Motion Chevy supercars since 1967. The last Baldwin-Motion Chevelle produced was this 1973 SS. It was powered by a seriously modified L88 427 that put out more than 550 horsepower. The king-kong engine, special body striping, aftermarket mag wheels, and side pipes helped run the original selling price up to a whopping $12,030—a gigantic sum in 1973.

◀ *1973 BUICK*

GS

All General Motors intermediates were restyled for 1973, but retained the 116-inch wheelbase. Buick resurrected the Century name for its version, and the GS built upon the Colonnade coupe. The 455 was available on all Century coupes, but the Stage 1 was a GS exclusive. Priced at $546, it had 270 net horsepower via a hotter cam and heads, Quadra-Jet carb, twin-snorkel air cleaner, and dual exhausts. Only seven were built with manual transmission; all others had the THM 400 automatic. Though not as potent as earlier Stage 1 Gran Sports, Buick's new edition was among the rarest, with just 728 built. The basic GS package added $173 to the Century coupe's $3057 list price. Special badging and handsome five-spoke wheels were included.

▼ *1973 OLDSMOBILE*

4-4-2

The Oldsmobile Cutlass put its own stamp on GM's Colonnade platform via unusual flared-out bodyside character lines and a split grille that wrapped under the front bumper. The 4-4-2 package added the FE2 "Rallye" suspension, which consisted of heavy-duty stabilizer bars front and rear, beefier rear upper control arms, stouter springs, and 14×7-inch wheels. To look the part of a muscle car, 4-4-2s also got a louvered hood, bolder segmented grille, bodyside and hood/decklid stripes, and 4-4-2 badges. The option added $121 to a base or Cutlass S coupe. This Viking Blue example has the top Cutlass engine choice: a four-barrel, 250-hp 455-cid V-8.

▼ *1973 OLDSMOBILE*
HURST/OLDS

The Hurst/Olds took a breather after 1969, but Hurst and Oldsmobile got back together again to make a new Hurst/Olds for 1972. The 1973 edition turned out to be the most popular Hurst/Olds yet, with production topping 1000 units for the first time. Ebony Black was now available as an alternative to Cameo White, and the 250-hp L75 455-cid big-block was standard.

▼ *1973 PONTIAC*
TRANS AM

The 1973 Trans Ams were the first to wear the giant "screaming chicken" hood decals. A Trans Am running the SD-455 engine could accelerate to 60 mph in less than 5.5 seconds and run the quarter mile in as little as 13.8 seconds, even with an automatic transmission—astounding for this era of declining performance. Plus, both Formula and T/A balanced their big blocks with wide tires and stiff suspension, so handling was quite competent for the day. Both were among the few really hot cars left.

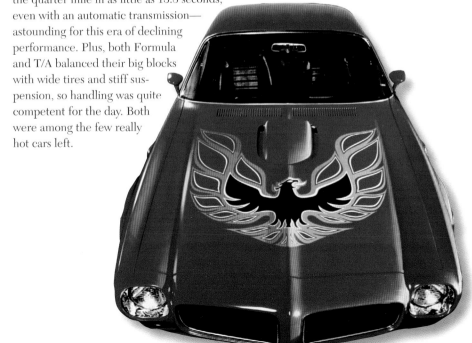

▲ *1973 PONTIAC*
FIREBIRD FORMULA

Firebirds were still wearing the basic look introduced for 1970, and performance-minded buyers could still choose from Formula or Trans Am models. The muscle era may have been winding down, but that didn't stop Pontiac from introducing the surprisingly potent new Super Duty 455 engine. Initially rated at 310 hp, the number was later revised to 290. Among other goodies, the SD-455 had a stronger block, four-bolt main bearings, forged rods, and TRW pistons.

▲ *1973 PONTIAC*
GTO

The once-mighty GTO was fading by 1973. It remained an option package for the redesigned base and Sport LeMans coupe. Despite an included 400-cubic-inch V-8 and heavy-duty three-speed floor-shift transmission, the '73 model was much less convincing than the GTOs of just a few years before. Among the few visual distinctions from the GTO's LeMans brothers were an NACA-scooped hood, blackout grilles, and specific grille and bodyside emblems.

▼ *1974 CHEVROLET*
CAMARO Z28

The 1974 Camaros sported stronger new bumpers front and rear, a redesigned grille, and "sugar-scoop" headlights and parking lights. Federally-mandated five-mph crush regulations meant that the split-bumper RS nose was history. The Z28 was powered by a solid-lifter 245-horsepower 350. Bold hood and decklid stripes were a $77 option that was not for bashful types; about half of the 13,802 Z28s built for 1974 got them. The Z28 would go on a brief hiatus after this year, returning as a separate model midway through the 1977 model year.

▲ *1974 OLDSMOBILE*
HURST/OLDS

It was back to "the Brickyard" for Oldsmobile and Hurst for 1974 with another Indy 500 pace car program (the first was in 1972). As was becoming common, that included a run of street replicas; these were again based on the Cutlass S. W-30 markings indicated that a 230-hp, 455-cid engine was underhood. A 200-horse 350-cube V-8 could now be had as well. The vinyl strip across the top of the street versions was intended to serve as a visual link to the targa band that helped protect the structural rigidity of the two Hurst/Olds coupes converted to open cars for actual pace-car duty. Many of the 380 replicas built were actually used in the Indy fleet, though not necessarily on the track.

▲ *1974 CHEVROLET*
LAGUNA TYPE S-3

The SS package was no more for 1974, leaving the role of the sportiest Chevelle model to the Laguna Type S-3. It was available with two- or four-barrel 350-cid V-8s, or a 235-horsepower 454. The big block was capable of mid-16-second ETs at around 87 mph—competitive for the era, but still disheartening. Starting at $3951, the Type S-3 came with a body-colored rubberized front fascia, swivel bucket seats, 15×7 Rally wheels, and special shocks. Chevy built 21,902 for 1974, and most of them were Antique White with Dark Red vinyl roof, interior, and accents.

▼ *1974 PONTIAC*
GTO

The name was the same, but the image, and most of the performance, was gone. Based on the ho-hum Ventura compact—a Chevrolet Nova clone—the GTO was a mere shadow of itself by 1974. Only 7058 Venturas were built with the $195 GTO option package, which included a distinctive grille, "shaker" hood scoop, and a 350-cubic-inch V-8 rated at 200 horsepower. Purists bemoaned the 1974s, recalling the days when GTO stood for driving excitement. Pontiac dropped the name after this year, but would revive it 30 years later.

1974 PONTIAC

FIREBIRD & TRANS AM

For 1974, the Firebird was deftly restyled to accommodate the new federal "crash bumpers" without ruffling its great-looking feathers. The facelift added a "shovel-nose" Endura front end with Pontiac's traditional split grille, and larger taillights. The 290-hp Super Duty 455 remained optional, though it found its way into only 943 cars, just 212 of them with a stick shift. Sales spurted upward for 1974, a bit surprising in light of higher fuel prices resulting from the Arab oil embargo. A total of 73,729 Firebirds were built, including a record 10,225 Trans Ams.

► *1975 CHEVROLET*

LAGUNA TYPE S-3

The sporty Laguna Type S-3 got a Camaro-inspired slope-nose front fascia for 1975. Slotted covers gave the opera windows a racier look. NASCAR racers appreciated the new nose, as it provided appreciable aerodynamic benefits on the big superspeedways. The 454-cid V-8, downrated yet again to 215 horsepower, made it into 1975 as a Chevelle option, but this would be its last go-around. It was not available in California or, curiously, the Laguna Type S-3, and the optional four-speed stick was no longer offered.

▲ *1976 PONTIAC*
FIREBIRD FORMULA

The 1976 Firebird Formula boasted a new appearance package that featured bold FORMULA graphics along door bottoms and rocker panels. Incorporated into a full-length, blacked-out strip, this suggestion of ferocious intent enhanced the mid-range model's attraction for customers who couldn't afford a Trans Am. Pontiac made a point of promoting a Formula painted Goldenrod Yellow in its ads, with black lower-body striping. The Formula also got a new hood with twin hood scoops set further back than before. The specially finished Keystone Rogue aftermarket wheels seen on this prototype were not a regular production option.

▲ *1977 CHEVROLET*
CAMARO Z28

Enthusiasts applauded the return of the Z28, which was revived midway through the 1977 model year as a stand-alone model instead of an option package. The $5170 price tag included a raft of performance and image goodies, including sport suspension components, front and rear spoilers, and dual exhaust. Color-keyed wheels and bumpers, body striping, and blacked-out grilles and headlamp/parking lamp bezels further added to the exclusive look. Handling was as sharp as ever, but the 185-hp 350 didn't provide the spirited acceleration of past Z28s.

▲ *1976 PONTIAC*
TRANS AM

Trans Am lost its 455-cube V-8 for 1975, regained it for '76, then dropped it for good after that. Base price for this '76 T/A was $4987. The 455 was a $150 option. The top engine provided decent performance, with *Motor Trend* driving a '76 455 T/A to low 16-second ETs and a 120-mph top speed. Sales steadily grew as Trans Am's rivals disappeared: 46,701 T/As were built for '76, 68,745 for '77, and 93,341 for '78.

▲ *1977 PONTIAC*
TRANS AM

Rectangular quad headlamps made their appearance on a sleeker Firebird front end for 1977, and were continued on the visually identical 1978 model. The 455 disappeared from the options list, making the 180-hp 400 and the 185-hp 403 the largest V-8s available. The Trans Am's popularity got a huge boost when it was featured in the hit 1977 Burt Reynolds movie *Smokey and the Bandit*, which was second only to *Star Wars* as the top-grossing film of the year.

▲ 1977 PONTIAC
CAN AM

For 1977, Pontiac whipped up a special appearance and handling package for the LeMans Sport Coupe that suggested an updated GTO Judge. Indeed, a print ad for the Can Am implored readers to "Remember the Goat!" Under the shaker hood was either the 200-hp 400 V-8 or, for California and high-altitude counties, an Oldsmobile-sourced 403 V-8 with 185 horsepower. Also included in the $5419 base price were power front brakes, variable-ratio power steering, front and rear stabilizer bars, and Pontiac's RTS handling package teamed with GR70-15 steel-belted radial tires on "whiteout" Rally II wheels. All Can Ams wore Cameo White paint with red/orange/yellow trim and a Grand Prix-style dashboard.

▲ 1979 OLDSMOBILE
HURST/OLDS

The Hurst/Olds popped up again for 1979 on the recently downsized Cutlass Calais coupe. The only engine was a 170-hp Olds-built 350 labeled "W-30" and linked to the THM-350 automatic with the traditional Hurst Dual-Gate shifter. All the H/O trimmings added $2054 to the price of a Calais. Though arguably the least special Hurst/Olds, the '79 found a warm reception, Olds building 2499. Of these, 1165 were mainly white, and 1334 primarily black. The gold two-toning treatment was standard. T-tops were optional, and a power sunroof could be ordered.

▼ 1978 CHEVROLET
CAMARO Z28

For 1978, the eight-year-old Camaro body got its second and final major facelift. Energy-absorbing body-color front and rear bumpers, larger taillights, and plusher optional interiors were among the changes. The Z28 was little changed mechanically, but gained more flash via front-fender vents and a duct-shaped hood scoop. "It'll put butterflies in your stomach, a lump in your throat, and a smile on your face," proclaimed one ad. *Car and Driver*'s four-speed test car did 0-60 in 7.3 seconds and covered the quarter mile in 16 seconds flat at 91.1 mph. Z28 prices started at $5604, and production hit 54,907.

▼ 1979 PONTIAC
10TH ANNIVERSARY TRANS AM

Firebirds were facelifted for 1979, gaining a new front fascia with separate quad headlights inset above low-mounted grille openings. On Trans Ams and Formulas, the new full-width tail-light panel featured a smoked-glass look that glowed red only when the taillights were illuminated. The Trans Am 10th Anniversary package featured a two-tone silver and charcoal paint scheme with special emblems and striping, and a custom silver interior with shag carpeting and other special trim bits. With a list price of $10,620, the 10th Anniversary T/As were the first Firebirds to top $10,000; 7500 were built.

◄ *1980 PONTIAC*
TRANS AM

The Firebird's 1979 facelift was carried over with little change for the 1980 models, but there were big changes under the hood. Engine offerings were cut dramatically, with the 350-, 400-, and 403-cubic inch V-8s all discontinued. The biggest Firebird mill was now a Chevy 305, rated at a lackluster 150 horsepower. However, Pontiac stepped up with a new turbocharged version of its 301-cid V-8, which put out a respectable-for-the-day 210 horsepower. Both Trans Ams and Formulas could get the turbo engine; cars so equipped could be identified by their asymmetrical hood bulges with "Turbo 4.9" callouts. The hood bulge housed a neat readout panel with a progressive turbo-boost indicator.

▼ *1981 CHEVROLET*
CAMARO Z28

GM's second-generation Camaro and Firebird entered their final year in 1981. The Z28 was little changed, although power was down somewhat from its previous 190 hp. The '81's standard engine was a 165-hp 5.0-liter (305-cid) V-8 teamed with four-speed manual transmission. Optional at no extra cost was a 174-hp 5.7-liter (350-cid) V-8 with automatic transmission; the four-speed manual was unavailable with the larger engine. Z28 production for '81 was a respectable 43,272. But that was still a considerable drop from its 84,877 high to this point, achieved in the 1979 model year. The 1981 Z28 had a base price of $8263.

▲ *1982 CHEVROLET*
CAMARO Z28

A 1982 Z28, still Camaro's performance leader, fronts its second-generation predecessor in this Chevrolet PR photo. The new car was 7 inches shorter, 3 inches slimmer, and fractionally lower on a new 104-inch wheelbase. Weight was down by 500 pounds. The standard Z28 engine was a rather mild 5.0-liter four-barrel V-8 that put out 145 horsepower. Outside of California, where emissions were more stringent, Z28 buyers hungrier for more could select a throttle-body "Cross-Fire Injection" version of the 305 small block rated at 165 hp and available (at first) with automatic transmission only. The standard Z28 V-8 could be teamed with either a four-speed manual or three-speed automatic.

◀ *1982 CHEVROLET*
CAMARO Z28

Designers aimed to give the 1982 Camaro an all-new look while continuing certain identifying styling cues such as single side windows, wide rear roof pillars, and broad tri-color taillights. Base price for the Z28 was $9700, and some 65,000 were sold. Many road-test reviewers of the day lamented the new Z28's middling power (a five-speed Z28 took 17.5 seconds to cover the quarter mile for *Road & Track*), but all agreed that its cornering ability and overall handling were outstanding.

▶ *1982 PONTIAC*
TRANS AM

The Firebird shared the Camaro's redesign for 1982, and Trans Am had the same power choices as the Z28. The Pontiacs got a more-aerodynamic (and distinctive) look via pop-up headlights and available smooth wheel discs. Pontiac advertising boasted that the '82 Trans Am's .34 drag coefficient was "the best of any production car GM has ever tested." Trans Ams didn't stand out as much from other Firebirds as before, but they did wear exclusive rocker panels and an offset hood bulge, among other exclusive trim bits.

◀ *1983 CHEVROLET*
CAMARO Z28

Powertrain improvements were the order of the day for the 1983 Camaros. The standard Z28 transmission was now a five-speed manual, while the outdated three-speed automatic was replaced by a four-speed overdrive unit. Horsepower was nudged up in all '83 Camaro engines. Late in the model year, a 190-hp high-output four-barrel 305 V-8 with a hotter cam and higher compression replaced the Cross-Fire engine as a Z28 option.

▲ 1983 CHEVROLET
MONTE CARLO SS

Chevrolet revived the SS moniker on a special-edition Monte Carlo that debuted midway through the 1983 model year. The Monte Carlo SS wore a slicked-up, droop-nose front fascia that helped its race-car counterparts compete against the aerodynamic new Ford Thunderbirds on NASCAR superspeedways. Not since the 1969-70 Dodge Charger Daytona and Plymouth Superbird had a car been specifically styled for NASCAR competition. Due to a late debut and manufacturing problems with the plastic nosepiece, '83 production totaled just 4714 cars.

▼ 1983 OLDSMOBILE
HURST/OLDS

The $1997 Hurst/Olds package included a showy hood bulge and rear spoiler, plus an eye-catching black-over-silver paint scheme accented by Hurst/Olds emblems and plenty of red striping. Handling was improved via uprated springs and shocks, sway bars, and special steering gear. While not quite as athletic as its lighter ponycar contemporaries, the 1983 Hurst/Olds could hold its own in a straight line, going 0-60 mph in around eight seconds and doing the quarter in about 16.

▼ 1983 OLDSMOBILE
HURST/OLDS

After taking a few years off, the Hurst/Olds returned for 1983 as a limited-edition Cutlass Supreme coupe. The revived '83 marked 15 years of Hurst/Oldsmobiles, and just 3001 were built for the model year. Standard engine was a 180-horsepower 307 V-8 with a four-barrel. Automatic transmission was standard, topped with Hurst's unusual (and somewhat gimmicky) Lightning Rod shifter. Mimicking the Pro-Stock drag-car shifters of the day, it had three levers: a main one, along with two separate sticks for manual shifting of first and second.

▲ 1984 BUICK
REGAL T-TYPE

GM's staid Buick division experienced an unexpected performance renaissance in the Eighties. The Buick Regal's major facelift for 1981 included a sloping hood and nose that made the car quite popular with NASCAR teams. Meanwhile, street-going Regals were available with ever-improving, surprisingly potent turbocharged 3.8-liter V-6 engines. The 1984 Regal T-Type's V-6 put out 200 horsepower and 300 pound-feet of torque.

▼ *1984 BUICK*
REGAL GRAND NATIONAL

The 1984 Regal Grand National was a mechanical twin to its T-Type sibling, but got an all-black paint scheme for a particularly menacing look. Vector style wheels added to the sinister vibe. *Motor Trend's* test GN did 0-60 in 7.5 seconds and the quarter in 15.88 seconds. The base price was $13,400, and just 2000 were made for the model year.

▼ *1985 CHEVROLET*
CAMARO IROC-Z

The big news for the 1985 Camaro Z28 was the introduction of the IROC-Z package. The IROC-Z commemorated the International Race of Champions series, which featured some of the world's best drivers competing in identically prepared race cars—Camaros, of course. Fitted with deep "ground effects" body cladding, chassis enhancements, and 16×8 alloy wheels, IROC-Zs came with a choice of the high-output four-barrel V-8 with five-speed manual or the new 215-hp tuned-port fuel-injection (TPI) engine with four-speed automatic. (The latter was also an option for the Z28.) Zero-to-60 was measured at an impressive 6.8 seconds, the quarter mile at 15.3 seconds at 89.1 mph, and skidpad grip at a neck-straining 0.85g.

▲ *1984 PONTIAC*
TRANS AM

Pontiac celebrated Trans Am's 15th anniversary in 1984 with a specially trimmed limited-production model. The anniversary package carried a hefty $3499 price tag, but it included the four-barrel 5.0-liter HO V-8, Recaro seats, leather-wrapped steering wheel, and a special handling package that included Trans Am's first 16-inch wheels. An all-white paint scheme with blue accents kept pace with the popular monochromatic "Euro-look" of the day and also recalled the colors of the original T/As. Just 1500 15th Anniversary Trans Ams were built: 1000 with automatic transmission and 500 with manual.

▲ *1986 CHEVROLET*
MONTE CARLO SS

A Monte Carlo SS "Aerocoupe" bowed for 1986. Its primary purpose was to homologate a more-aerodynamic rear window for use in NASCAR superspeedway racing; Chevrolet said that the wind-cheating wraparound window cut the SS's coefficient of drag ratings from 0.38 to 0.365. On street-going Aerocoupes, the window made for a slicker profile but also a much-smaller trunk opening than a regular notchback Monte SS, as this side-by-side comparison illustrates. Power for the Aerocoupe came from a high-output version of Chevy's 305-cid small-block V-8. Fitted with a four-barrel carburetor and high-lift camshaft, it made 180 hp.

▼ *1986 PONTIAC*

2+2

Pontiac followed the Monte Carlo SS Aerocoupe's formula with an aero-nosed fastback variant of its Grand Prix. Dusting off a performance name from the Sixties, Pontiac dubbed it 2+2. In addition to the wraparound rear window and unique urethane nose, all 2+2s wore a unique silver-over-charcoal paint scheme with specially finished Rally II wheels. Handling enhancements included stiffer springs and beefier sway bars. Pontiac produced just 1225 2+2s.

▲ *1987 BUICK*

GRAND NATIONAL

Buick produced its last rear-wheel-drive Regals for 1987, as an all-new "GM10" front-drive model was being prepared for 1988. Sadly, that meant the end of the road for the already-legendary Grand National models. For 1986, Buick added an intercooler to its turbo V-6. By '87, the GN's turbo V-6 was up to a healthy 245 horsepower and 355 pound-feet of torque.

1987 BUICK

GNX

Buick decided that its Regal GNs deserved an especially grand send-off, so it cooked up the ultimate Grand National: the limited-production GNX. Just 547 were built, at a sticker price of $29,290 (though red-hot customer demand often pushed actual transaction prices higher). A bigger turbocharger and intercooler, along with other enhancements, gave it 276 hp. *Car and Driver*'s test GNX did 0-60 in 4.7 seconds, the quarter in 13.5 at 102 mph. Among factory 1987 cars, only Porsche's $106,000 911 Turbo Cabriolet could match the GNX's acceleration. Other GNX upgrades included a transmission oil cooler, Stewart-Warner analog tachometer, composite fender flares and functional front-fender vents, and upsized VR-rated tires on 16-inch BBS-style wheels.

▶ *1987 OLDSMOBILE*

4-4-2

The Hurst/Olds was replaced by a reborn
4-4-2 after 1984. The same 307-cid V-8 carried over, with power ratings little changed at
170-180 horsepower. *Car and Driver* drove
a 1985 4-4-2 to a 16.6-second ET at 83 mph,
and went 0-60 in 9.1 seconds. The swan-song
1987 model, shown here, was a $2577 option
on the Cutlass Supreme coupe. About 4210
were sold. For 1988, the Cutlass moved to
GM's new front-drive "GM10" platform.

◀ *1987 PONTIAC*

FIREBIRD FAMILY

This 1987 Firebird "family portrait" shows
off the differences among the base Firebird
(background), Formula (left), Trans Am
(right), and the line's new flagship, the Trans
Am GTA (foreground). In addition to such
appearance items as a revised spoiler and
rocker skirts, the $2700 GTA option included
the biggest V-8 to be found under Firebird
hoods in years: a tuned-port-injection 5.7-liter
lifted from Chevy Corvette. Rated at 210 hp
at 4000 rpm, the 5.7 delivered an impressive 315 pound-feet of torque to the rear
wheels. The engine received an oil cooler to
ease its high-action strain, while the driver
slipped into a fully articulating seat to ease
the pain on long journeys. Also included:
P245/50VR16 tires on gold cross-lace wheels,
the WS6 performance package, and four-
wheel disc brakes.

▼ *1989 PONTIAC*
20TH ANNIVERSARY TRANS AM

Pontiac never passed up the opportunity to trot out a special-edition model for Trans Am's milestone anniversaries. The 20th anniversary model was extra special, it was essentially a GTA powered by the turbocharged 3.8-liter V-6 from Buick's recently departed GNX. In the Trans Am, the turbo V-6 was rated at 250 horsepower and 340 pound-feet of torque. One of the most potent Trans Ams ever built, the 20th Anniversary model came only with an automatic transmission. The all-white body was adorned by nothing more than subtle "20th Anniversary" cloisonné emblems and "Turbo Trans Am" badges.

▲ *1991 PONTIAC*
TRANS AM GTA

Pontiac gave its ponycar a facelift in the spring of 1990 and labeled it a '91 model. The cosmetic changes were inspired by Pontiac's Banshee concept car. All four Firebird models—base, Formula, Trans Am, and Trans Am GTA (shown here)—received new front and rear fascias and smaller headlamps. Trans Am and GTA also sported fresh taillamps and shared new bodyside skirting. Not everyone cared for the new look; the "beaky" new nose was especially controversial. The Trans Am's standard powerplant was a 230-hp 5.0 V-8, with the 240-hp 5.7 optional.

1992 CHEVROLET
CAMARO Z28

Camaro turned 25 in 1992, and Chevrolet commemorated the occasion with a $175 Heritage Appearance Package for both RS and Z28 models. Included were nostalgic hood and decklid stripes and a decklid badge. The Heritage Appearance Camaros also served as a send-off to the long-running third-generation Camaro, since the redesigned fourth-gen car was just around the corner. Good thing, too, since Camaro suffered a 30.6-percent decline in total sales for 1992. Despite its robust powerplants and flashy add-on styling pieces, the basic Camaro design was showing its age.

◀ *1992 CHEVROLET*

CAMARO RACING

Camaro's racing credentials were always rock solid, so it was natural to pose the 1992 Z28 with its "then and now" road-racing relatives. The blue car is Penske Racing's all-conquering 1968 Sunoco Camaro, the car that captured the '68 SCCA Trans Am championship. The light-orange car is Scott Sharp's Duracell-sponsored SCCA Trans Am Camaro. Unlike the '68, this car was a purpose-built, tube-chassis machine that shared virtually nothing with a factory-stock Camaro.

1993 CHEVROLET

CAMARO Z28

The all-new fourth-generation Camaro debuted for 1993. Its wheelbase stayed the same, but the car was slightly heavier despite more extensive use of plastics. The interior was all-new, and got vastly improved ergonomics. Anti-lock brakes debuted as standard equipment. The big news underhood was a new LT1 5.7 V-8 with 275 hp, 30 more than the previous engine. *Motor Trend* drove a six-speed '93 Z28 to a 14.0-second ET at 98.8 mph. Sticker prices started at $16,779. The new Camaro was a logical choice for the 1993 Indianapolis 500 pace car, and Chevy offered 645 limited-edition replicas for retail sale. Here, the '93 pace car poses with its '67, '69, and '82 forerunners.

▶ *1993 PONTIAC*
TRANS AM

All-new Firebirds arrived with the same basic design as Chevy's '93 Camaro, but retained a unique Pontiac style. For 1993, both came in hatchback coupe form only; convertibles weren't offered until '94. Pictured here is the Trans Am, which used the Z28's 275-hp 5.7-liter V-8. A new six-speed manual transmission was also standard in Trans Ams, along with specific bucket seats, a performance axle ratio, and Z-rated 16-inch tires. Base price for the '93 Firebird Formula was $17,995; the Trans Am was $21,395. Overall Firebird production for '93 was a low 19,068.

▼ *1994 PONTIAC*
25TH ANNIVERSARY TRANS AM

To no one's surprise, Pontiac issued yet another special trim package in 1994, this time to celebrate Trans Am's 25th anniversary. The $995 option included white alloy wheels and leather upholstery, blue stripes, and unique badges. Anniversary Trans Ams started at $22,504 for the coupe, $27,964 for the ragtop. Among Trans Am drivetrain revisions for '94 were a forced one-to-four skip shift on the manual trans and, late in the model year, optional traction control. In tests of an automatic-transmission 25th Anniversary Trans Am convertible, *Car and Driver* did the quarter mile in 14.6 seconds and clocked top speed at 153.

▲ *1994 CHEVROLET*
IMPALA SS

To the delight of big-car performance fans everywhere, Chevrolet resurrected the Impala SS name for 1994 on a hot-rodded Caprice sedan. Exterior cues included a subtle rear spoiler, restyled "dogleg" rear-quarter windows, and a unique blacked-out grille. The standard power-plant was the 260-hp 5.7-liter LT1 V-8 that was optional on other Caprices. Also included were a sport suspension, 17-inch Z-rated performance tires on distinctive five-spoke alloy wheels, and front bucket seats. Any color was available, as long as it was black.

► *1996 CHEVROLET*

CAMARO Z28 SS

The Camaro Z28's LT1 V-8 was up 10 horsepower to 285 for 1996, thanks in part to more-efficient sequential fuel injection. If a 285-hp Z28 wasn't enough, buyers could also choose a new Z28 SS with a 305-hp LT1, unique hood with functional forced-induction hood scoop, upgraded suspension, and 17-inch Corvette ZR-1-style wheels. Though the $3999 SS package was available through Chevrolet dealers, the modifications were actually performed by aftermarket tuning specialist SLP Engineering of Troy, Michigan. Testifying to its quality, the SS carried the same factory warranty as any other Chevy, though SLP offered to cover its own modifications for a separate but equal three years/36,000 miles.

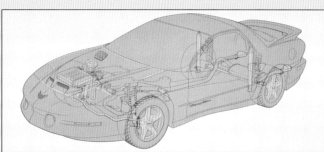

1996 PONTIAC

FIREBIRD FORMULA AND TRANS AM

V-8 versions of the Firebird were also bumped to 285 horsepower for 1996. Formula and Trans Am models were available with a $2995 WS6 Ram Air Performance and Handling package that included stiffer springs, 17-inch tires, and a ram-air induction system that boosted engine output to 305 hp. The ram-air system required a new hood with dual scoops. The illustration shown here highlights the WS6 package's components in yellow on a Trans Am (note the round inset fog lamps in the front fascia). Formulas (left) had a slightly more subdued nose with simulated air inlets instead of fog lamps.

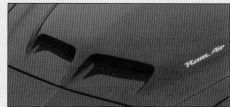

◀ *1997 CHEVROLET*

30TH ANNIVERSARY CAMARO

Chevrolet got in on the anniversary special-edition act again in 1997, for the Camaro's 30th. Available on both coupes and convertibles, the 30th Anniversary package included Arctic White paint set off by eye-popping Hugger Orange stripes on the hood, roof, and tail, plus black badging and white 16×8 five-spoke aluminum wheels. The paint scheme was a tip of the cap to the 1969 Camaro Indy 500 pace car, and also mimicked the look of the 1996 NASCAR Brickyard 400 pace car. Available cloth seat inserts picked up the nostalgic houndstooth pattern that was optional on 1969 Camaros. All 1997 Camaros wore 30th Anniversary headrest logos and sported a redesigned, more-ergonomic dashboard.

▶ *1998 PONTIAC*

FIREBIRD FORMULA WS6

The biggest news for 1998 GM ponycars was the LS1 V-8. This aluminum 5.7-liter engine was introduced the previous year in the Corvette, replacing the original 1955-design Chevrolet small-block V-8. Although an overhead-valve design as its predecessor was, the LS1 had practically nothing else in common with it. Along with the engine change came another boost in power for the Camaro Z28, Firebird Formula, and Trans Am: All gained 20 hp, to 305. Power increased by 15 for Ram Air and SS packages, to 320 hp. With the new engine, the top '98 F-body models took their place among the quickest muscle cars ever. *Motor Trend*'s '98 Ram Air Trans Am ran a 13.4 quarter mile at 107.3 mph.

▲ 1999 CHEVROLET
CAMARO SS

Camaros were facelifted for 1998 with a more sculpted nose, composite headlights, and a larger, more menacing grille opening. The 1999 models were mostly unchanged. A Z28 SS convertible like the one pictured here would set a buyer back at least $32,085: $28,385 for the car and $3700 for the SS package. Sales for GM's ponycars were slipping quickly as the Nineties wound down; Chevy moved around 136,000 Camaros for 1995, but only 43,000 or so for 1999.

▼ 2002 CHEVROLET
35TH ANNIVERSARY CAMARO

The end of an era: While 2002 marked the 35th anniversary of the Chevrolet Camaro, it was also the last production year for both General Motors F-body cars. The farewell-edition Camaros came only as red SSs, in either convertible or T-top coupe form. Included in the $2500 package were silver checkered-flag-pattern stripes, special fender badges, embroidered headrest logos, and ten-spoke SS wheels with machine-faced surfaces and black accents. After 35 continuous years of production, the Camaro was gone. Bow-tie fans lamented the loss, but as it turned out, Camaro's disappearance was only a hiatus.

▼ 1999 PONTIAC
30TH ANNIVERSARY TRANS AM

Pontiac again went with a nostalgic white-with-blue-stripes paint scheme for the special-edition 30th Anniversary Trans Am, but also threw in unique blue-tinted wheels. Production was limited to just 1065 coupes and 535 convertibles. The anniversary baubles added $1575 to the $26,175 base price of a Trans Am coupe or the $30,245 tab for a Trans Am ragtop. The $3150 Ram Air Performance and Handling option was mandatory.

▼ 2002 PONTIAC
COLLECTOR EDITION TRANS AM

By 2001, sales of the Pontiac Firebird had fallen to about 21,000 units annually. The Ford Mustang was outselling both the Camaro and Firebird by better than three to one, and General Motors wasn't putting much future development into its ponycars. These factors led GM to make 2002 the last year for the Firebird. The send-off Collector Edition Trans Ams wore black wheels and bright-yellow paint with special stripes.

▼ *2004 CADILLAC*

CTS-V

A Cadillac muscle car might seem like something of an oxymoron, but GM's flagship division rolled out a hot-rodded sports sedan for 2004 that exhibited many of the traits of a classic muscle machine. The CTS-V carried serious muscle in the form of a 400-horsepower version of the Chevrolet Corvette's 5.7-liter V-8, linked to a mandatory(!) six-speed manual transmission; no automatic was available. Brembo brakes and a sport suspension helped provide handling on par with the power. *Car and Driver* achieved a 4.8-second 0-60 time and ran the quarter mile in 13.2 seconds at 109 mph in their CTS-V test car.

▲ *2004 PONTIAC*

GTO

The fabled GTO name made a surprising return to Pontiac's stable for 2004. Aside from rear-wheel drive and thumping V-8 power, the new GTO shared nothing with the legendary Goats of yore, being an Americanized version of the four-seat Holden Monaro coupe from GM's Australian branch. A split-grille Pontiac face and badging were the only real external differences between the Monaro and the GTO. Under the hood was a 5.7-liter LS1 V-8 that packed a healthy 350 horsepower and 365 pound-feet of torque.

▲ *2006 CHEVROLET*

CAMARO CONCEPT

Chevrolet axed the Camaro in 2002, citing waning sales as the reason. In 2005, Ford's redesigned, retro-themed Mustang became a runaway sales success, reinvigorating the ponycar market and spurring Chevy to resurrect the nameplate it had abandoned three years prior. The striking Camaro Concept was unveiled at the 2006 North American International Auto Show in Detroit. The showstopping concept drew styling cues from the iconic 1969 Camaro, and packed a 400-hp LS2 V-8. Fans cheered when GM boss Rick Wagoner announced in August '06 that Chevrolet would build a production version.

▼ *2004 PONTIAC*

GTO RAM AIR 6 CONCEPT

Despite its impressive performance and classy interior trimmings, the new GTO's lack of aggressive performance-car design elements severely hampered its sales. Most muscle-car fans decided that it just didn't look enough like a GTO. Pontiac spiced things up nicely with the Ram Air 6 concept car, but unfortunately its styling enhancements wouldn't see production. A new twin-scoop hood and 6.0-liter V-8 were added for the '05 models, but they weren't enough: The GTO was dropped in '06, after just three model years of disappointing sales.

◀ *2008 PONTIAC*

G8 GT

For 2008, Pontiac again tapped GM's Australian connection, this time to create a new large sedan with genuine muscle-car spirit. The Pontiac G8 was a restyled, Americanized version of the Holden Commodore VE. Rear-wheel drive and the availability of a strong V-8 were part of the Aussie platform. Base G8s came with a respectable 256-hp 3.6-liter V-6, but true performance fans were drawn to the G8 GT: It carried a 6.0-liter V-8 with 361 horsepower.

▶ *2009 CADILLAC*

CTS-V

Cadillac introduced the second-generation CTS-V as a 2009 model. It upped the ante in every way over the already formidable original CTS-V. Under the hood was a 556-hp supercharged and intercooled 6.2-liter V-8 cribbed from the Chevrolet Corvette ZR1 but modified for added quiet and smoothness. GM's sophisticated Magnetic Ride Control suspension system was standard; it used magnetically-charged fluid instead of mechanical shocks to improve both ride quality and cornering ability.

◀ *2009 PONTIAC*

G8 GXP

For 2009, the Pontiac G8 lineup gained a top-dog GXP model with a 415-hp version of the 'Vette's 6.2-liter V-8. Sadly, one of the best high-performance Pontiacs ever would also be the last; all G8 production ended soon after the April 2009 announcement of the Pontiac brand's imminent cancellation. G8 GXP production totaled a mere 1824 units. Of them, 981 were fitted with automatic transmission and 843 with the six-speed manual. With that, the marque that essentially created the muscle car as we know it was history.

▶ *2010 CHEVROLET*

CAMARO SS

After three years of anticipation and hand-wringing speculation, the reborn Camaro finally went on sale in the spring of 2009 as a 2010 model. The high-performance SS models ran with a version of Corvette's 6.2-liter V-8; the mill was rated at 426 hp with the six-speed manual transmission, or 400 with the extra-cost six-speed automatic. A faux nose scoop situated just above the grille opening was an SS-only styling feature. SSs also got uprated FE3 suspension, Brembo brakes, and a limited-slip differential.

◀ *2010 CADILLAC*

CTS-V

By 2010, the Cadillac CTS-V family had grown to include rakish coupe and station-wagon models, both with the same fire-breathing 556-hp V-8 as the sedan. The examples shown here wear a mid-2011 special appearance package called the Black Diamond Edition. It included special "SpectraFlair" metallic-black paint, Satin Graphite-finished wheels with yellow brake calipers, and Recaro seats. Most CTS-V road tests returned 0-60 times in the low-four-second range and quarter miles in the low 12s.

▶ *2011 CHEVROLET*

CAMARO SS

To no one's surprise, a drop-top variant joined the Camaro model roster for 2011. Well-engineered internal reinforcements and bracing created an impressively solid body structure, which made convertible Camaros almost as nimble as their coupe siblings. Though true muscle aficionados opted for the copious V-8 muscle of SS Camaros like this one, even base models were surprisingly gutsy. For 2011, Camaro's 3.6-liter V-6 got an eight-horsepower boost, to 312 total.

2012 CHEVROLET
CAMARO ZL1

Spurred by ever-improving Ford Mustang high-performance models like the Boss 302 and Shelby GT500, Chevrolet honed the new Camaro into a true racetrack-ready machine. The 2012 Camaro ZL1 was named for the limited-production super Camaros of 1969, and it lived up to its namesake and then some. Under the hood was a variant of the supercharged LSA V-8 used in the Cadillac CTS-V. In the ZL1, it was rated at 580 horsepower at 6100 rpm and 556 pound-feet of torque at 3800 rpm. In addition to the serious horsepower infusion, the ZL1 got massive 20×10-inch front- and 20×11-inch rear wheels, Brembo brakes, Magnetic Ride Control, and GM's Performance Traction Management. The PTM system integrated traction control, stability control, and power-steering feedback, and could be set to one of five modes to suit driving conditions varying from wet-road driving to full-bore track laps. The ZL1 started at $54,995, not including the requisite gas guzzler tax.

▶ *2013 CHEVROLET*
CAMARO ZL1

The Camaro ZL1 debuted as a coupe only, but droptop versions were set to follow later in the 2012 calendar year—they packed most of the same functional performance upgrades as the coupes. GM engineers spent a lot of time in the wind tunnel with the Camaro ZL1 in order to maximize the car's downforce while minimizing drag, which produced a number of special components on the production car. The hood was aluminum, with a carbon-fiber center section and a large vent that relieved engine-compartment air pressure and heat. The aggressive front fascia used an integral air splitter for downforce, and belly pans underneath the car helped minimize airflow turbulence and aid transmission cooling.

THE FUTURE

The 21st-century muscle-car fight starts Round Two when the three contenders are redesigned in response to fast-moving market changes, escalating federal fuel-economy standards, and new safety and environmental regulations. Current intel indicates the sixth-generation Camaro will start sale in fall 2015, more than year behind the new 50th Anniversary Mustang, though it will doubtless be previewed for many months before that.

Today's fifth-generation Camaro uses a cut-down version of the "Zeta 1" architecture developed by General Motors' Holden branch in Australia and which featured on the 2008-09 Pontiac G8 midsize sedan. The 2016 Camaro will move to the company's new rear-drive Alpha platform that premieres with Cadillac's long-awaited BMW 3-Series fighter, the compact 2013 ATS sedan. Though some sources suggest little change to Camaro's overall size, trade weekly *Automotive News* reports that GM planners have been wrestling with every aspect of the redesign. "GM views the current car as a big success," *AN* observes, "and the automaker is cautiously taking steps to avoid—well, let's call it screwing up…"

Like today's Chevy ponycar, the sixth-generation is coming together under the direction of Camaro chief engineer Al Oppenheiser. The styling team is again led by Tom Peters, GM's design director for performance cars.

Oppenheiser told *AN* that planners are dealing with three main issues. The first is weight: "We always get hammered for mass, and that's not going to be getting easier going forward" with rising fuel-economy standards. Then there's the engine lineup: "Displacement, number of cylinders, all of these things you need to think about." The final challenge, unsurprisingly, is styling. "Do you make it look like a second-gen [1970-81 Camaro]" or "like the first gen [1967-69]?" That last point may be telling, as today's Camaro pays homage to the classic '69 design without copying a single line.

Though Team Camaro isn't about to tip its hand this early in the game, the Alpha platform is apparently much lighter than initially reported, which could make weight-watching a bit less stressful for Oppenheiser and company. But regardless of how much fat is lost, we suspect the exterior package will be trimmed to some degree, possibly close to that of today's Ford Mustang or even a bit smaller, perhaps on the order of the first-gen or downsized 1982-92 Camaros.

As for engines, several sources believe choices will begin with a four-cylinder or two, likely sized at 2.0-2.5 liters and probably turbocharged. Forced induction may also be available for a step-up V-6 that should be an improved version of GM's already excellent 3.6-liter twin-overhead-cam design. Finally, Camaro's V-8 is almost sure to become smaller and more efficient than today's 6.2-liter. We'd look for something on the order of 5.0-5.5 liters, again with optional supercharging. This engine could be basically the same one being rumored for Chevrolet's next-generation C7 Corvette. If so, it should be

virtually all-new with the possible exception of retaining overhead-valve cylinder heads for reasons of lower cost and easier underhood packaging, not to mention maintaining Chevy small block tradition.

Whatever the final choices, all next-gen Camaro engines will doubtless maximize mpg with features such as direct fuel injection, "double" variable valve-timing (intake and exhaust), and low-friction internal components. There's also a good chance of GM's eAssist "mild hybrid" electric drive being standard or optional across the board. Ditto turbocharging for the four and V-6.

Transmissions will also be chosen to provide a competitive balance among performance, fuel economy, and refinement. There's talk of new 7-speed manual and 8-speed automatic for V-8 and uplevel V-6 models, but we think it more likely that GM will stick with its current pair of 6-speed trannies, at least for the sixth-generation's first couple of years.

Though longtime muscle-car addicts may despair at the prospect of smaller engines with less power, the sixth-generation Camaros are doubtless being developed for weight-to-power ratios at least on par with those of today's models. That means performance should be as strong as ever, and possibly stronger. The big question is whether rising CAFE (corporate average fuel economy) tar-

gets could spell the end of big-power engines like the new ZL1's and make, say, 400 hp the new normal for future muscle cars. If today's horsepower race does continue, it will only be because GM, Ford and Chrysler will keep boosting the horse counts, knowing they can't afford to let up and the other guys have hp bragging rights. The downside, of course, is that Detroit won't be able to sell as many such cars as the market might want. Even then, they'll have to move a lot of very thrifty small cars to offset the fire-breathers' toll on CAFE numbers.

Rounding out the technical story, the next-gen Camaro is sure to inherit the Alpha platform's four-wheel independent suspension with coil springs, front struts, rear multilink geometry, and front/rear antiroll bars, though with many or all components redesigned to suit the ponycar package. Like today's Camaros, the new ones will boast good-size 4-wheel disc brakes with ABS and integrated stability/traction control, plus beefy wheels and tires. Steering assist will probably go from conventional engine-belt-driven hydraulic to electrohydraulic or pure electric, again to maximize mpg.

Styling? Our Thom Taylor illustrations assume that Chevy will take an evolutionary approach with a more-expressive interpretation of today's car. But regardless of what

themes are invented and/or followed, the new Camaro is bound to retain traditional long-hood/short-deck proportions and a low, wide stance. Surfacing and details will hinge on final exterior size and whether sales trends suggest the need for a big departure from today's aggressive sharp-edged look. Ed Welburn, GM's Vice-President of Global Design, is an avid Camaro fan, so he's probably urging Tom Peters' team to strive for a blend of familiar elements and fresh touches—and to improve aerodynamics as another aid to fuel economy.

The 2016 Chevrolet Camaro will continue the rapid rejuvenation of Chevrolet's car line that began with the new-for-2008 midsize Malibu. The results have been uniformly impressive, but no less so than General Motors' remarkable recovery from the depths of its historic 2009 bankruptcy. Freed of

Thom Taylor's future Camaro renderings draw several cues from classic 1969 Camaro design elements; notice the squared-off wheel openings and their accompanying bodyside character lines. The tri-segmented headlights are a clever riff on the '69 RS model's headlight covers, while the hood bulge hints at the '69's Cowl Induction hood. The interior features a modern rendition of the first-generation Camaro's stirrup-shaped console shifter, and updates the '69's "twin-binnacle" gauge arrangement with a swooping shroud reminiscent of the fourth-gen Camaro.

crushing "legacy" costs, and having gone through a painful organizational restructuring, today's GM is a much leaner and more competitive automaker that is back to making money for its shareholders and great vehicles for its customers.

GM's new-found vitality bodes well for the next-generation Camaro. Though it's bound to be somewhat different from the ponycar it replaces, we have little doubt that it will be another winner. Here's to the future!